Building

Black Belt Business

By

Michael Turbitt

Is this book for you?

If you are like most Martial Artists I have come across, who want to pass on their knowledge to others, you will have devoted several years of your life to learning and practising a Martial Art; and now feel it is time to give back to others, and, with a bit of luck, perhaps start to recoup some of the financial commitment you have made over the years. It is time to start a Club.

When you do, you will, most likely, be moving into uncharted waters, and into the realms of renting rooms or leasing properties, holding public liability and other insurances, setting the level of training fees, arranging bank accounts and accountants, marketing to attract students, creating websites……. the list goes on and on. Whichever way you look at it, what you are really starting, is not a 'Martial Arts Club' but a Real World Business. In my words, a Black Belt Business.

I am not sure how much money you have spent over the years in learning your Art; the fees for your instruction, the courses you have attended, the travelling to events or competitions, the clothing and equipment you have purchased - not to mention the value of your time that you have spent getting to this point. The financial investment you have made, I have no doubt, runs into several thousands of Pounds, Dollars Euros or whichever currency you utilise.

And don't get me started on the Blood, Sweat, Tears and Knocks that you have surely endured over the years. I know, you have already made significant investment in your Martial Art to be where you are today.

But I would like to ask you a question.

How much Time, Money, Blood, Sweat and Tears have you expended during the last few years, on learning how to run a Real World Business?

If the answer is like that of the majority of Martial Artists who want to start a Martial Arts Club is 'Little to None' then I have written this book **specifically for YOU.**

Learning that your 'head guard' is not adequate can result in a painful lesson, but learning about Business the hard way is definitely not something I recommend. It is frustrating, stressful, very expensive and worst of all it can make you fall out of love with the thing you love the most. Your Martial Art.

This is the time to invest a few of your hard earned Pounds Dollars or Euros, and a little of your time into learning about how to build a successful Black Belt Business.

If you learn just one thing from this book which makes a difference to your Black Belt Business, it will out-weigh the cover price thousands of times over, and in the long run, may just help save your sanity.

Contents

IS THIS BOOK FOR YOU?	2
CONTENTS	4
ACKNOWLEDGEMENTS	11
WHO THE BLEEP IS MICHAEL TURBITT	14
"I would pay to train ....and teach for free!"	14
DON'T READ THIS BOOK!	23
CHAPTER 1 FIRST PRINCIPLES	25
1.1 What is Money? Could it be Chickens?	25
1.2 What value can I give?	30
CHAPTER 2 THE BLACK BELT BUSINESS MIND SET	34
2.1 A New Perspective requires New Thinking	34
2.2 More Money Equals Lower Standards!	36
2.3 One in a Thousand...	37
2.4 Respect your students!	40
2.5 The two most important sentences in this book...	41
2.6 It's Your Black Belt Business	43

CHAPTER 3 YOUR BLACK BELT BUSINESS LOOK LIKE?   47

3.1 What will your Black Belt Business look like?   47

3.2 Why would you do this?   47

3.3 What do you do?   51

3.4 OK. What else matters to you about what you are doing?   54

CHAPTER 4 TARGET MARKET   57

4.1 Target Market   57

4.2 Point of View   60

4.3 So a drop in standards then?   61

4.4 Who is Your target market?   64

4.5 Most of your Customers Most of the Time   68

4.6 Add this to your vision   73

CHAPTER 5 HOW WILL YOU TEACH WHAT YOU TEACH?   77

5.1 Sorry, but *these* are really the most important sentences in this book!   77

5.2 Paul McCartney   79

5.3 Now Add this to your Vision Statement   82

CHAPTER 6 DOES IT MAKE SENSE TO YOU?   84

6.1 Just a Quick Check   84

6.2 Will your answers give you what you want from your business?   85

6.3 Your Answers, Your Business!   86

6.4	Actually, I think *this* really is the most important sentence in this Book.	88
6.5	Just for reference.	89
6.6	DO THIS!	91
6.7	The Mission Statement for Team Black Belt	93

CHAPTER 7   LOCATION, LOCATION, LOCATION   98

7.1	Location, Location, Location	98
7.2	LOCATION	98
7.3	Location 2	100
7.4	Your own Venue	102
7.5	Location 3	103

CHAPTER 8   SHOW ME THE MONEY   107

8.1	Important Sentences.	107
8.2	What's a lesson worth?	109
8.3	Show me the Money	110
8.4	The Real Reason for charging more:	114
8.5	What are your Martial Arts lessons worth?	115
8.6	Fee structures	116
8.7	How many lessons a week should your students attend?	117
8.8	Additional family member Discounts?	119
8.9	Pay as You Go or Monthly Collection?	119
8.9	These are the most important sentences in the book!	122

CHAPTER 9   KEEPING IT A SECRET!   124

9.1   Yes more important sentences!   124

9.2   Get Clear   125

9.3   They Ain't Bothered   130

9.4   Your Identity   134

9.5   Have a credible website   135

9.6   If a picture says a thousand words, a video might say a million.   137

9.7   Testimonials   138

9.8   About Us (yawn)   138

9.9   Website Rankings   139

9.10   Social Media - DO IT!   140

9.11   YouTube   140

9.12   Other Advertising   141

9.13   Press Advertising   141

9.14   Editorials   142

9.15   Marketing - to sum up   143

CHAPTER 10   PROGRAMMES AND STRUCTURE.   144

10.1   Complementary Programmes   144

10.2   Class structure   145

10.3   STOP IT!   147

10.4   So, how long is a lesson?   149

10.5   Class Control   150

10.6	Eight year old Black Belts. What the...... !!!	151

CHAPTER 11 ROTATING CURRICULUM 155

11.1	What is a Rotating Curriculum?	155
11.2	Advantages over Traditional	156
11.3	How to Create a Rotating Curriculum	157
11.4	Is it worth it?	161
11.5	Gradings - Everyone Passes!	162
11.6	What about Black Belt Gradings?	164

CHAPTER 12 CONTROL YOUR BUSINESS 167

12.1	Business Dashboard.	167
12.2	So what are the key indicators I need on my dashboard?	168
12.3	Information the Easy Way	170

CHAPTER 13 BUSINESS PLANNING 171

13.1	Your Vision	171
13.2	5 Year Dream	171
13.3	One Year Objectives	175

CHAPTER 14 BUSINESS STATUS 185

14.1	What kind of Company will you be?	185

CHAPTER 15 THE MOST IMPORTANT SENTENCES. 188

CHAPTER 16 .... AND ONE MORE THING! 202

ADDENDUM 205

INDEX 207

Acknowledgements

This is my first book and as I started to write, it became crystal clear to me that I am, not as my ego would like to believe, someone that I have created - I am not solely responsible for who I am and what I do. As I've worked through this book it is evidently clear that I am a product of the people with whom I have shared my life, the people to whom I have aspired, and to those who have lifted me to do better.

I want to thank those people, and I want to express how grateful I am to be what they have helped me to become.

I want to thank my parents, whose hard work and efforts to make my childhood as good as it was possible for it to be. Mum, Dad - thank you. I had a fantastic childhood. I saw you working two and three jobs to support us and to pay for us to have the best we could. I noticed when you gave me the good bread and you picked the blue bits off yours, even though you didn't want me to see.

I learned the lessons of generosity, hard work and self-sacrifice.

Thank you.

I want to thank the people in my Martial Arts life - these are the people who I tried to emulate. I want to thank the instructors and training partners for their efforts and energy, but you gave me more than that, you gave me your belief that I could achieve, I could do better, and I know without you I might not have been able to.

I want to thank Sensei Graham Tuckey, a great influence on my early Karate life and Sensei Ian McCrannor, with whom I tried to keep up. Thanks as well to Sensei Diane Jarvis and Sensei Doug Sedgley, my long suffering practise partners.

Sensei Les Giles, who, after I had taken a rest from Martial Arts, invited me to re-join the fold and helped me get back to doing the thing I loved, and special regard and thanks to Sensei Nigel Davison, without whom Team Black Belt would just not exist. Your help and inspiration is greatly appreciated. I have trained all over the world with so called experts - Sensei Davison you are Truly World Class. Thank you.

To my partner, Helen. I know you, (to misquote a famous Julia Roberts' line), "Rescued me right back". You hold things together. You support me, encourage me, and occasionally kick me, but most of all you love me. I am grateful for all of those. You are a full partner in my life and in Team Black Belt and I know you have my back, and so much more. Behind every great man is an exhausted woman… I know!

Thank you Helen. I love you.

To my children. I love you, and it gives me great pleasure to watch you develop into the adults you are becoming. Please stop trying to give me a heart attack!

To Dawn, my ex-wife, thank you. Our business life did get in the way much of the time, but things forged in a furnace become extremely strong. You and our children have been a fantastic part of my life, I wouldn't have swapped it for the world. Done a few things differently, sure, but never swapped it.

I have saved Sensei Barry Tatlow until the end; always there for me from the day I was born, to my first Karate lesson, to the text messages I receive today.

I was once asked "Who has been the most influential person in your life?" My answer was instantaneous: My Uncle Barry.

You are the one who took me from being a Child to being a Man, my guiding path, through you teaching me Karate and through the pub based lessons on how to conduct myself.

I haven't always shown the respect I should have, and for that I apologise, and for the grace you have shown in 'forgetting' those times, I am in total awe.

To my Uncle Barry… Thank you.

Who the Bleep is Michael Turbitt, *and why has he written this book?*

"I would pay to train ....and teach for free!"

I really would. I expect most Martial Artists out there are the same. I love what I do. I want to get better and I want to pass it on to others.

Although this book is about how to run a Black Belt Business which makes money, all I really want to do is to give back to students.

I want to allow others to feel as good as I did the day I passed my Black Belt; to get the huge amount of joy and the fantastic feelings of achievement, success, confidence and strength which being involved in Martial Arts has given me and to be able to develop the friendships which so far have lasted half of a lifetime.

It is my contention that the core beliefs, values and the physical practice of Martial Arts are extremely valuable in today's society, far beyond any monetary value that I can place upon it and far above the value of other activities or interests (and of much more value than a Satellite TV Sports Subscription!).

I have never been, and now will never be, a World Class Martial Artist. I can claim no World Records or

Championships, nor, as a matter of interest, can footballer Sir Alex Ferguson, (Manager of Manchester United), but what I strive to be now is a World Class Teacher and a World Class Instructor in the world of Martial Arts.

I thank you for taking the time to at least peek into the cover of this book, and if, like me, you strive to be a better teacher and provider of Martial Arts to others, I invite you to read the rest.

I was born just before Karate arrived in the UK in the early 60s, and I started training in 1973, as an eleven year old.

Then stopped.

The Dojo was no place for a child - it was a hard place to be.

Fortunately, the Instructor, Sensei Barry Tatlow, was my Uncle. He was one of the first in England to train with Sensei Tatsuo Suzuki in one of the first Dojos in the country (in Ravelles Gym, Temple Passage in Birmingham).

My Uncle had set up a Dojo in Coventry (the first in the city) in order to, afterwards, as so many Instructors did, train and practise with others in the hope that his teaching would pay for his own tuition with Sensei Suzuki.

My Father was one of Sensei Tatlow's first students, and I have included a picture overleaf of the two of them from the very early days of Karate in the UK.

With all that family involvement, it wasn't too long before I re-joined the Dojo of Sensei Tatlow. (He still trains and teaches in the location today, some 50 years on.)

In 1981 I gained my First Dan whilst still training with Sensei Tatlow, who was at that time affiliated to Sensei Takamizawa (whose name I am proud to say is on my certificate). I also went on to gain my Second Dan two years later, again awarded by Sensei Takamizawa.

I subsequently opened, and shortly afterwards, closed, my first Karate school, and set off on the journey towards family life.

I was, by now, married, and had left my engineering 'Job for Life' with Jaguar Cars Ltd to work in a Recruitment Agency, recruiting engineers for other companies.

After a row with a boss, (I still think he was wrong), I decided to start my own recruitment business. As a good friend of mine is fond of saying, "How hard can it be?"!

Bloody hard - that's how. However I was determined, and had two daughters to provide for. Together with my then wife, we built up a company with twenty full time staff, employing over three hundred temporary and contract workers. We turned over £5 million at our peak with offices in 5 cities.

God I hated that business. Stress and hassle, dealing with other people's problems, clients bitching all day long, contractors needing chasing up, the Banks trying to sell me money when I didn't need any, and taking it back off me when I did.

It did however have compensations apart from the financial benefits. I was controlling a complex, people-based company, and although at the time I didn't appreciate it, I was learning a lot about life, human beings and even more about how to run a business.

I was learning about hiring people, training them, setting performance targets for them, nurturing them, motivating them, rewarding them, and, yes, firing them if required.

I was learning about the Premises Leases, the Landlords and Tenants' Act, Property Dilapidations, Service Charges, hidden fees, Solicitors, (don't get me started on Solicitors), Contract Law, Hire Agreements, rental and purchase laws.

Learning about European Working Time Directives, Employment Law, VAT, dealing with HMRC, Accountants, Limited Company Status, Partnerships and Pensions, Employment Rights, and Statutory Sick pay, Employee holiday entitlement and, of course, Maternity leave.

Breathe, ready, go..

Key Performance Indicators, how to hold meetings, how to sell, how to market - and to whom. I learnt I shouldn't spend thousands of pounds on stupid things like advertising on the back of buses! Duh!

How to budget and to calculate my profit, read a balance sheet and talk the strange foreign language of Accountants. I learned to predict my cash flow into the business, and I learned what to do if an employee stole £34,000 from the business. (There was some arse kicking done in the payroll office that day.)

I learned what to do if someone was taking me to court and I learned how to take others there.

Karate Training was just not a viable option for me with a business and family - now with a son as well as two daughters.

But I was learning how to set up, start and run a business - none of those lessons have been wasted or forgotten. I wasn't training in karate terms, but I was training for what I do now - running a Black Belt Business.

Then in 2002 the inevitable happened - Divorce. I was single again and I had a much smaller business, which became even smaller after a client went bust owing us just shy of £250,000. There were interesting business lessons learned that day too.

Ah well, there is always Karate.

So off I go, invited back by a friend, Sensei Les Giles of Sparkhill Karate School, into proper training again as part of the Wado Academy, with Sensei Shiomitsu at the top.

I was also training with a friend of mine. His school was part of Sensei Barry Tatlow's Phoenix Karate Organisation, and had been established 16 years earlier. (This school had seven students, and was to play a key role in my story). I was training with Sensei Tatlow too, back in my old stomping ground!

After training quite seriously for the next 2 years, I was getting back in shape and the next part of my story unfolded; a chance meeting with Sensei Nigel Davison leading to an invitation to visit his Northampton based Dojo.

I walked in. My life changed, there and then, in a heartbeat.

After twenty years of running a business I hated, after taking personal development course, after personal development course, after endless business courses, expansion plans and business set-backs, after searching my brain for something I wanted to do with my life - there it was...

It was the freshest, brightest, cleanest Dojo I had ever seen.

The lessons were full of students getting a fabulous quality of instruction in high energy classes, and were totally engaged; sweating, learning and grinning from ear to ear.

I'm a business man and I don't do tree hugging but a thought passed through my brain, a thought that changed my life:

This is what I was born to do!

Ten days after that day at Sensei Davison's Dojo, my friend running the club with seven students told me he was planning to close the club in a few week's time. Well it didn't close – instead it was the start of my remarkable journey.

I was now a Karate Instructor with seven students and if this was what I born to do, then I had better get good at it. Not just better at it, more than better; I wanted the students who put their energy, time, money and above all, trust, in me, to have a reason for doing so.

I felt the responsibility to ensure that what I taught, and the way I taught it, was the very best I could do. I set my goal, to become a World Class Martial Arts Instructor, and, that, as they say, is how my journey began.

I now run, as Principal Instructor, Team Black Belt Karate School; with 300 students training over four nights a week at a single venue Dojo in the Midlands, UK.

I know how to run a Business and I know how to teach Martial Arts.

Does one devalue the other?

In my opinion the opposite is true. Being a Professional means I can give more energy and time with better instruction, to more people; with methods which are better thought out, in a better environment with greater focus than an Amateur Martial Arts teacher can realistically hope to achieve.

Am I World Class?

Not yet. But, as it is an immeasurable goal, I just have to try to be better this week than I was last, and next week I aim to be better again.

Over the years, I have seen some extremely competent Martial Artists who were never able to pass on their knowledge and experience to others, because they didn't have the business knowledge that would have empowered them to do so.

It is my hope that the contents of this book will mean you won't be one of them, that it will give you the business knowledge, structure and practices which will enable you to create the fantastic Black Belt Business which currently resides in your head.

Enjoy.

Sensei Barry Tatlow (My Uncle), and Jack Turbitt (My Dad) circa 1967 Holbrooks Dojo, Coventry, England.

Don't read this book!

When I say don't read it, I mean don't *just* read it; it's a workbook, a 'fill in the blanks' kind of book, an interactive book. If you're about to read it on an E reader, you will need a couple of sheets of paper and a pen (I know - so old fashioned).

Someone once said "the quality of the answer depends upon the quality of the question". Or did I just make that up? Anyway it's true. The answers you arrive at will surely depend upon the questions you ask. So in this book, as well as giving you 'My' take on things, I will ask you to give, and write down, 'Your' take on things. After all, it will be your Black Belt Business not mine, so your answers are the ones you will need.

I will ask you to focus on the Business outcomes as well as your Martial Art outcomes.
I will get you to question your current beliefs and the way you do what you do; whether you can improve the content, the style or effectiveness of what you're doing?
Whether you can you get better in areas you are weak? Not in the Martial Arts sense; I am not concerned with your Round House kick; I am concerned with business things, such as the appearance of your Dojo; whether or not you can pay yourself a living wage or whether more students leave than you can attract in any given period.

So, by all means feel free to use this book as a reference book, but please, please do more than that. Get involved with the questions and use it as a tool to make things better for you and your students.

If you disagree with the things I say, hey that's ok; it's your life and your business. If you do disagree however, ask yourself if it's you who disagrees, or is it conditioning from your previous instructors from the last century?

Chapter 1   First Principles

1.1   What is Money? Could it be Chickens?

So I typed 'what is money' into Google.

Zero point Two One Seconds later there were Five Thousand One Hundred and Seventy Million answers available. That's a lot of talk about money.

I want to use a definition I heard recently which made sense to me.

Money is a way of exchanging value. Simple eh?

I don't know what the other 5,169,999,999 were talking about; waffle mainly I suppose.

You see in the old days, before there was money, if you wanted your house (hut) fixing you would exchange a chicken in return for the work being carried out.

So it went something like: One day house fixing = One chicken

Now if your hut was in a really bad way: Seven days house fixing = Seven Chickens.

When the guy who fixed your hut wanted to obtain a new axe head, he might exchange Two Chickens with the axe maker in return.

Oh the ease of it all. A Chicken here and a Chicken there.

A Chicken came to represent a value, whether it was a day's house building or half an axe. Life was good, but there were a few problems.

"What if you didn't have any Chickens?" I hear you ask! (Go on - ask)

"What if you didn't have any Chickens?"

Thanks, I told you it was an interactive book didn't I?

Well, you might have a few Cabbages to trade with, or you might trade your time because you were able to weave Baskets, and so on.

So to make it clear, 3 Cabbages might equal 1 Chicken which equals 6 hours weaving or one day's house fixing! Simple.

(You needed very big pockets in the old days!)

There had to be a better way…..

So along comes some bright spark who invents MONEY.

Money represented the 'value of things to be traded'. The more Chickens the trade was worth the more money you got instead.

It still works as it always has done; things have a value to you and that value is represented by little coins or notes or numbers in your bank account.

The more house fixes you do, the more money (Chickens) you receive.

The next two sentences are the most important sentences in this book.

Money is the Representation

Of Value,

the more Value you Give the

more Money you Receive.

You can't Earn Money,

you can only Give Value

and in Return you

Receive Money..

1.2 What value can I give?

Ah I'm glad you asked, because that's the question, I mean the real question, the BIG one. If you can answer that you have cracked it.

Martial Arts has **MASSIVE** value to give.

Look at the world around you; it's full of numpties with no morals, taking from the world, causing trouble, bitching about others, bringing people down, energy sapping, brain numbing, jealousy ridden self-centred, ill mannered, lying, cheating bast....ds.

And that's just the celebrities the population looks up to!

Come on! Martial Arts is the antidote to this stuff. We are disciplined, considerate, honest and with integrity. We aspire to better ourselves and help others. We are positive and creative. I needn't go on; just ask yourself what are you like at your best, and where do those influences come from?

Value? Don't talk to me about value. Martial Arts are needed now more than they ever have been, not because we have to defend ourselves more often - we don't - but because of all the values and beliefs that doing Martial Arts can give.

1.3 How do I give Value, and so, receive money?

Black Belt Business gives Value and receives money, in several ways:

1   Lessons

In this, the exchange of your knowledge, enthusiasm, skills, beliefs and principles which you pass on to students is directly rewarded by them paying a mat fee. It is a fair exchange.

You are teaching something extremely important and extremely valuable. Your lessons should not be cheap, otherwise you devalue your hard work, effort and what you and Martial Arts has to offer.

2   Gradings

You give Value to your students when you Grade them. Their hard work and concentration is tested by you and then they are rewarded by confirmation that they have done well, that they are on the right track and that they are progressing towards their goal.

You could just give them a belt, yes, but it is not the same as taking a formal test. Give them that test that challenge and facilitate the great feelings which go with rising to meet it. It has a Value to them; in return you deserve to get a financial reward back. Charge for your Gradings.

3   Membership

Membership fees are an important part of them joining a group. People like to be liked and like to be accepted as part of a group. You cannot teach everyone in your city, you have a very select number of students, you must treat your Black Belt Business as if it were a special exclusive place to be a member.

How much is it to join a golf club, for heaven's sake? People pay thousands of pounds so they can hit a ball around a field; the more expensive it is to join, the more special they think it is.

If you are prepared to accept them as students into your Business then they should feel special. Remember the old Masters who would not train people until they had proven themselves worthy to be trained?

You cannot these days make them perform some test of worthiness, as a sign that they are committed and serious about training it seems reasonable these days to charge a membership fee. (should you wish to waive it in special circumstances or special hardship you can, it's your Black Belt Business).

4   Clothing

As with the last section, clothing gives students a feeling of belonging to something special: tee shirts, track suits, the 'Club' Badge.
(I will not use the word Club again in this book, please forget that word exists.)

5 Equipment

You are helping people to improve themselves, helping them move towards their goals, there is a Value in that.

It's more convenient for a student to buy 'approved items' from you than track down, their own stuff and take the risks that it is rubbish when it arrives. That service has a Value to them and it probably means it's more inconvenient for you! So charge them accordingly.

Can you discount the stuff you sell to them so they get things a bit better that retail? It's entirely up to you. I do, it creates good will and puts them on your side.

6 Events, Courses and One Offs

These are great Value to students whether it's more training or more learning or just more fun. You will soon know if it is of no Value to them: they won't come.

So, the above are some of the main ways you can give value to your students. Don't be ashamed of doing so; if you give Value then you should expect Chickens in return and most people want to give you the right number of Chickens for the right amount of Value. If not, they will start to feel in a mental debt, they'll know they are not paying enough for what they are getting, and will feel uncomfortable. People are funny like that.

(As an aside, I have found that if I place a high monetary value on something, it makes me work harder and perform better, so that I know in my heart of hearts I am still giving **value for money**).

Chapter 2 The Black Belt Business Mind Set

2.1 A New Perspective requires New Thinking

A new perspective means a new way of thinking, which, at this moment, neither you nor your Martial Art may be comfortable with. As this book is entitled 'The Black Belt Business', I am going to offer my thoughts on the business aspects of Martial Arts. However, in order for you to get the most out of this book, it is my advice that you make a conscious decision to free your mind from the objectives (and possibly constraints) of your Martial Arts system, Chief Instructor or Association and its inherent practices and/or procedures, and allow yourself to give your personal financial outcomes at least equal, if not more, significant billing.

I appreciate that for many Instructors, to change the way things have always been done, may be considered by some as 'disrespectful' to your Chief Instructor, Teacher, Association or style etc, and therefore may be a difficult process to undertake. I would certainly not encourage any Martial Artist to disrespect the people who have nurtured them thus far.

However it is my contention that all Martial Arts are constantly changing, evolving and growing; Kung Fu is no longer the sole practice of temple dwelling monks, Karate no longer the sole domain of the Okinawans born before 1920 and so on. In order to operate in a modern society and in a 21st century business environment, it is necessary to at least 'examine' if the way things have 'always' been done can be improved, modified, upgraded or added to, in order to provide a meaningful training experience and a financially viable Instructor.

As a Martial Artist since 1978, I understand the pressure to keep things the same, to follow and to be loyal. I appreciate that to start thinking about change can sometimes be challenging.

In order to get the best from this programme I would ask you to park the issue of 'what will the head of your Association or the Grand Master say if I do xyz' for a moment and, by using your experience, knowledge and expertise, design your own Black Belt Business.

Do I advocate throwing out all that has gone before? NO! Tradition is the basis for Martial Arts. Without at least recognising the past we risk creating a nonsense, a folly. Without listening to the lessons of the people who have studied Martial Arts for a lifetime we can stumble into the future ill prepared, and without the knowledge that is available.

However, I do want you to undertake the task of designing your Black Belt Business as if you had a free hand to change, modify and adjust anything you wanted, in order to have a successful business. Or, at the very least, imagine you've been tasked by your Chief Instructor to modernise and improve the professionalism of the way your whole group teaches, and with the full blessing of your peer group, you are to become a trail blazer for the whole group, style or association.

Let me now address the fear which inevitably raises its ugly head:

2.2   More Money Equals Lower Standards!

I am aware that many of the Professional Instructors have, shall we say, lower standards than some of us hope for; producing Black Belts which, to be honest, would struggle to hold a green belt in other groups. Remember however, producing poor students is not just the realm of the Professional Instructors; many 'Hobby Martial Artists' also produce poor results.

It is also true that many Professional Instructors are superb Martial Artists. They have dedicated themselves 'full time, for a lifetime' to their art and have produced teaching methods and training structures of the highest standard and therefore have also produced students who are consistently of fabulous quality.

In short, the amount of money you charge bears little relationship on the quality of the art, but can have a fantastic impact upon the quality of the teaching facilities, and create more opportunities for progression.

Just think for a minute. If you had trained in order to become an accountant, a doctor, a secondary school teacher, a lawyer or a skilled craftsman, for four, five, seven or even ten years; if you had dedicated every waking hour, every spare moment to obtaining a degree or similar trade qualification, if you had paid the financial cost of obtaining the relevant instruction, the social cost of spending hundreds of hours studying and the physical cost, in blood, sweat and tears, (literally in some cases), of getting to the required standard in your chosen profession; then you went out and took a job as a lorry driver, in order to keep your profession 'pure', (i.e. unsullied by financial reward), people would think (with some justification), that you were out of your mind. Your family would be mortified that you had thrown it all away. They would be right!

Do Jane Torvill and Christopher Dean lessen their Olympic brilliance by inspiring thousands to take up ice skating? Does Sir Alex Ferguson cheapen his leadership abilities because he is highly paid for doing it? Of course not.

Are you lessening your art by being paid well to teach it, to inspire hundreds of people to get off the couch and train in your type of Martial Arts....?

Should you not be rewarded for your ability to change lives, enhance society, to help the country's obesity epidemic, the lack of moral guidance for the young and old alike, and society's general apathy?

Martial Arts have a fantastic contribution to make in my humble opinion. If you do not have a successful Black Belt Business you darn well should have. A Black Belt Business which rewards you emotionally, spiritually and financially.

2.3 One in a Thousand...

If you are still not sure things may be in line for a change, let's have a quick look at the number of students who start Martial Arts to the number of students who achieve Black Belt status.

Throughout my Martial Arts career, I cannot recall the number of new starters I have seen come and go.

Thousands and thousands and thousands of potential Martial Art Black Belts wasted. Millions and millions of pounds in never-to-be-collected mat fees!

To tell the truth, I simply can't even remember the name of any Martial Artist who trained for less than 3 years and, in truth, probably five years.

If the government made you send your child to a school at which only one student in a thousand (or worse) passed a GCSE, the country would be in uproar; and yet a number of Martial Artists seem to take this kind of 'achievement' as a matter of pride. "Only the very best student gets to be good in my school!", they declare. Only the best students? We can all train the best students - almost anyone can teach a naturally gifted, highly motivated student ....

It's not a matter of pride that an Instructor has a school full of these students - it's a matter of shame.

These Instructors are likely to have a small number of ego based students, and the students are apt to take it upon themselves to start a competing Black Belt Business in the school 200 yards away, and try to steal any other naturally gifted students for themselves. Not a sound business model.

Some of the very 'old-school' schools I have seen also have a 'weed out' policy of mentally 'unsuitable' students. These are the students who aren't hard enough, i.e. those who won't do five hundred push ups to start the class, or put up with being kicked around – 'cannon fodder' I hear them being called; those students not committed to 'mastery' (repeating the same thing again and again and again, up and down a room like robots).

Only the dullest, mind-altered student would inflict themselves to attend some of the lessons I have seen taking place.

As a result of pompous, self-interested or misguided Instructors, thousands and thousands of students vote with their feet (and wallets) every year and leave Martial Arts classes.

We all know that if students are motivated to attend often enough, for long enough, nearly all of them can achieve a Black Belt. After all, the saying goes "a Black Belt is a White Belt who never gave up", and if you can't see your way to awarding a Black Belt to a student who has committed ten years of his life to training under YOUR instruction (and some can't), then what, exactly, have you been teaching them…?

The average student, or even the 'struggler', motivated and interested for the long term, may not be quite as rewarding to the ego as the Naturally Talented, Aggressive, Athletic, Six Foot Three, Twenty Three Year Old Student (who almost any Instructor could teach), but they are good for your business, and in the longer term, much more rewarding to help develop as human beings.

In today's society there are very few people who will persist with any activity that they don't love doing; there is simply too much out there competing for their attention, their interest, their time, their energy and their money.

2.4 Respect your students!

Your students will look up to you, admire you and treat you as a role model. One definition of respect that I use is 'having respect means treating people how you would wish to be treated'. I think for many Martial Arts Instructors that's exactly what they do.

However, if you are a product, as I am, of the 1970s and 1980s, treating people how you would wish to be treated or how you were treated back in the day, is a potential mistake. Your expectations of what is required may not match up with your students' expectations.

In the same way as you expect electric lighting in a Martial Arts school (as opposed to generations of old pre-World War 2 Masters), today's students expect a degree of customer service and training ethos which reflects the age.

Students expect Professional Instructors they can talk to, a training programme which is designed in line with their physical and mental abilities, the training undertaken to be motivating and uplifting, as opposed to a trial of stamina and strength, to be treated with courtesy and friendliness and not cold shouldered, to be accepted into the group and not to be forced to prove they are good enough to be in the school.

2.5 The two most important sentences in this book…

<u>If your Students do not love attending your classes they will go and do Something Else.</u>

If they do Something Else,

you cannot teach them

anything and

they will pay you

NOTHING!

2.6 It's Your Black Belt Business

As a new student to Martial Arts (all those years ago), you probably had some idea that the ultimate status in Martial Arts was the Black Belt. You may have had some idea that it was only given out to people who had mastered some kind of fighting, punching, kicking, throwing etc.

On your first visit to a Black Belt Business, this idea was probably confirmed and certain ideas you had were clarified. After a few lessons you may have been given the whole syllabus, in book form, or maybe just the requirements for the Yellow (first) Belt.

You were on your way; you had a beginning point, you knew how poor you were and just an idea of how good you were going to have to be.

You were going to be led through a process, a number of clearly defined techniques, and a number of clearly defined thoughts and moves, shown exactly what a great performance looks like, given immediate and direct (sometimes too direct) feedback on a minute by minute basis, and in the end, through a series of testing points and an examination, to reach your goal - your Yellow Belt.

Then again, through a process of clearly defined requirements to gain the Green Belt, more feedback, more examination against set criteria and so on and so on.

Until the day comes your Black Belt Grading Day... the greatest day of your life, even better than getting married or having kids - we know!!!

Well, you're at the beginning again. To run a successful Black Belt Business, you need to have a Black Belt Business Syllabus, a blue-print to follow, some idea of what you want to achieve and how you are going to achieve it. Which step are you going to take first, and what comes next. What else you need to learn, practice and develop. Where that will lead and so on.

So where is it? Who is going to give you the Black Belt Business syllabus?

The short answer is, in most cases, no-one, because there isn't one. But it might be a darn good idea to design one.

Designing your Black Belt Business Syllabus is what this book is all about.

The Business Syllabus is NOT the grading system you use for you and your students. I repeat, the Business Syllabus is nothing to do with which bits of their bodies your students have to wave and where they wave them to earn their next belt, it's way more important than that. It's your **Black Belt Business Success System**.

Will you always stick to your Business Syllabus? Probably not! It's your syllabus and your business, so you can write or re-write it as you wish, but it is an important starting and reference point.

Your Black Belt Business Syllabus will cover all the aspects of your Business.

Your objectives

What you want to give to others

What you want to get out of the business?

What you will or won't do

What you'll teach, and to whom

How you will control your business

Budget and finance

Legislation

Leadership development

Expertise

Standards

You are going to have to design a Black Belt Business Syllabus which meets your needs.

I will repeat that you are going to design a Black Belt Business which meets **YOUR NEEDS, YOUR VALUES AND YOUR BELIEFS.**

If you compromise at this stage you will regret it. You are going to live with this Black Belt Business, **YOUR** Black Belt Business.

It should be what **YOU** want it to be.

Where **YOU** want it to be.

When **YOU** want it to be.

How **YOU** want it to be.

Achieving for **YOU** the rewards **YOU** want to achieve. Teaching what **YOU** want to teach, how **YOU** want to teach it.

The aim of this book is to walk you through the design stage of your Black Belt Business Syllabus.

Chapter 3   Your Black Belt Business look like?

3.1   What will your Black Belt Business look like?

What is your Vision for the future?

In the first section of this programme I will be asking you to establish the vision for your business. Please note - not your *club*, your *hobby*, your *passion*, but your <u>business</u>. Your Black Belt BUSINESS.

Working through a small number of questions, (outlined below), will give you some clarity and enable you to have a focal point for your thinking, around which all of your business decisions can be made.

The answers to the questions will form the basis of your Black Belt Business, and the likely success thereof.

3.2   Why would you do this?

The biggest question before we go any further is why do you want to do this? Why do you want a Black Belt Business? What drives you to undertake this commitment? What's in it for you? Clarity at this stage will pay dividends later. What is the single most important thing to you, what has to happen to make it a successful venture? What is the primary reason for creating this Black Belt Business?

Later in the process this will become extremely useful, especially when choosing a direction for your teaching style and the outcomes you want for your students; for what you decide to do and not do in your Black Belt Business.

I understand there may be many reasons - financial, spiritual and philanthropic, all of which play a part; but right now, from the list below, I ask you choose YOUR PRIMARY reason for setting up your business.

(At this stage I want you to think like a White Belt; you know that people are successful and you think it might be cool to be like that, but you are not sure how or what it takes, or what work is involved, you just know you want to have a go. We will test your assumptions later in the book, so for now, just like the beginners in class, get stuck in and go for it!)

Choose your PRIMARY reason for setting up your business from the list below.

1   To pay for your own training (a common reason for starting a club).
2   To help pass on knowledge and benefits to others.
3   It's just the next step.
4   To promote the style.

5   Because it's expected by a higher grade or leader of my group.

6   To earn extra income for nice stuff. (How much in £'s per year.)

7   To replace a salary. (How much in £'s per year.)

8   To make a higher standard of living. (How much in £'s per year?)

9   To create a business. (Profit in £s per year, size in number of students?)

10   To make an empire or association. (Turnover in £s per year? Size in number of students?)

Or other reason…. If so what, and can you put a £ figure on it?

If you have answered from the top half of the list (1 to 5), whilst possibly highly admirable, you will have a hobby club, not a Black Belt Business. If you have chosen from the bottom section (6 to 10) it **doesn't** exclude the more philanthropic elements of the above in your motivators, (so you could have answered 1 to 5 as well), it is just you are thinking (in my humble opinion) like a Black Belt Businessman, and that's a **<u>Good</u> <u>Thing</u>**.

Before doing anything else, please write it down on the space below.

My answer to section one, my Primary Objective, is:-

....
....
....
....

Which earns me £..............'s per year.

"Hang on", I hear you cry, "What about the other stuff?"

Well, we will come to that; you don't have to bin it all in pursuance of the money.

Just for now, I want you to understand that the primary reason for any business is to make money. Sorry, but there it is. If you want to allow as many people as possible to get the massive rewards that you have obtained from Martial Arts, then the business must make enough money to support you and your family. If you just want to teach a couple of people on a Friday night then you have a hobby.

(And you are selfishly depriving hundreds or thousands of lives that could be improved by Martial Arts, in order to benefit the people or company that employs you during the rest of the week!!!!)

Sorry, off my soap box now.

3.3 What do you do?

What are the Objectives of Your School?

This is your vision, or at least the starting point of it.

What is the overriding objective of your Black Belt School? For some it will be to produce great competition fighters, for others it will be to offer a form of fitness training to the local population, or to improve the self belief and confidence in as many students as possible; and this would be reward enough.

Clearly, producing great competitive fighters will lead to improvements in self-confidence of the students. But a Black Belt Business which has the objective 'to increase self-confidence of students' may not, and I repeat, *may* not, produce any competition fighters; and clearly the training style needed for each type of student, would be vastly different. Your overriding goal for your school will determine the 'style' for your business.

So, I ask you to choose the primary overriding objective of the school. (If you don't have a single objective, place your top three objectives in order of importance and bear in mind the fewer objectives, the greater the clarity and clearer direction for your school.)

The main objective of the school is to produce....

Black Belts of the highest standards possible.
As many Black Belts as possible.
Elite competition fighters.
Kata/form/pattern experts.
Technical experts.
Good all-rounders.
MMA fighters.
Students with improved general fitness.
Art Form Mastery.
Street fighters.
Style perfection.
Student personal growth.
Improved self-confidence.
Self Defence experts.
Calm, stress free human beings.
Another objective.

My answer to 3.3 is: My school will produce

……..…..………………………………..…..………………………
………………………………………………………………………
………………………………………………………………………
………………………………………………………………………
………………………………………………………………………
………………………………………………………………………
………………………………………………………………………
………………………………………………………………………

Again, go back and prioritise other answers and of course, feel free to add any of your own. You may wish to 'play' with these objectives to see how these would pan out. It's only on paper, at the moment!

3.4 OK. What else matters to you about what you are doing?

You have the starting point of your Black Belt Business, the monetary value you require from the business and the primary objective of the school, now what else? What about the other values that you hold? I know you're not just in it for the money.

I know that if you are reading this book, you want to 'Do Some Good', you have some 'Give Back' in your heart, so what is it? Write it down so you can show someone what you and your business stand for.

What values will it hold? Will you cheat and steal or will you treat others with honesty, respect and integrity?

Will you give out belts to those who can give you £500 each time (some people's business model!) or progress people only on merit?

What about less able students? Should they go somewhere else to train or are they welcome if they do their best?

What's your business philosophy - what's important to you because it might be the thing that's important to your students?

What feelings did you get when you passed your Black Belt? Is that how you want others to feel?

You need to start to become very clear about your business and what it stands for, and now is the best time to do so.

If you were going to task someone else to create the business you have in your head, what words would you use, how would you ask them to behave, treat people, achieve? In short what would you ask them to create? This is your Vision.

The next few pages are designed to help you formulate YOUR vision for YOUR Black Belt Business.

In the space provided on the next page I want you to write down, in your own words, something like:

I will create a Black Belt Business which will....

in the next x years generate an income of £50,000 per year through the teaching of abc students to become experts in Self Defence by utilising our xyz style of Karate.

We will treat our students as.....

if all can achieve success, and we will support less able students.

We will create feelings of....

achievement, pride and self-worth etc.

Our Black Belt Business Values are....

Honesty, Clarity, Perseverance, Friendliness, Strength etc

Ok your turn. Complete the following:

I will Create a Black Belt Business which ....
....
....
....
....
....
....

We will treat our students as ....
....
....
....

We will create feelings of ....
....
....
....

Our Business Values are ....
....
....
....

If you need more paper...... do I really have to say this bit? If you want to reword rewrite or adjust the sentences, hey just do it! It's your Black Belt Business.

Even if you got no further forward than having these guidelines for your Business you would be way ahead of other Martial Arts Clubs or Black Belt Businesses.

Chapter 4   Target Market

4.1   Target Market

This is the most important sentence in this book (as well)....

<u>Your</u>

<u>Target Market</u>

<u>Dictates Everything</u>

<u>your Business does.</u>

I know, another one, but actually *this* just might be the most important sentence in this book……

Everything Should be

Aimed at Attracting

And Retaining

Your Target Market.

I will repeat that EVERYTHING, and I mean *EVERYTHING*, you do should be aimed at attracting and retaining your Target Market.

When your Grand Master is paying your wages every month, he/she can tell you how/where/when/and what to teach. Until then, with respect:

EVERYTHING you do should be aimed at **Attracting and Retaining** your **Target Market Customer**.

Can you keep your Grand Master happy, and so keep your soul?

The answer is yes, quite possibly. With good communication, and if he/she is going to get another 300 licences a year, they should be happy about it.

Remember though, it is your Black Belt **Business**, not your hobby, and not your Grand Master's hobby either. He won't be paying for your family's holidays this year; you and your Black Belt Business will.

If you can attract 300 new students to your business, it is likely that a percentage will want to do 'the full on, Grand Master, degree level' version of what you teach. Make a separate class for them, (charge them extra by the way), but you are now focusing on the needs, expectations and preferences of your Target Market to build your income.

4.2 Point of View

Your Target Market, the people you want to attract to your Black Belt Business, all have different expectations, demands, requirements and 'would like to have' ideas in their heads. They will have many differing reasons for starting a Martial Arts class, all valid, and all that will need to be catered for. They will see and do things from their own point of view and if you don't accommodate their point of view they will go somewhere else that does.

It is highly likely that you have a *different* point of view to a new beginner to a Martial Arts class. You may have been taught in the 'old way', as I was, with established teaching methods and ideas, and belief systems in your head which nowadays conflict with modern thinking.

I remember the 'Old Days'. Training in a Community Centre with solid block wood floors, (I know, you used to lie awake at night *dreaming* of solid block floors!) with some guest instructor who was intent on 'weeding out' weaker students - you know, the who ones who couldn't 'hack it'.

Demonstrating throwing techniques, and determined to show the technique several times - damaging the student with every throw. These Instructors were elevated to such a level that 'ordinary' students couldn't even talk to them. They were ferried about in limos and put up in hotels at the expense of the students, and treated with 'god-like' reverence. (Not that I'm bitter at all…..)

I felt that the contempt these 'Old School' Instructors had for their students (that were paying them), knew almost no bounds. They knew best and if the student didn't like it, they could leave....

Not the best retention tool I have come across.

This type of set up still exists today, still goes on. However, it is becoming less and less common, simply because holding this point of view doesn't pay, which nowadays it needs to. In the world of the Black Belt Business if it doesn't pay…… don't do it.

If your point of view is similar to the 'Old School' instructors, then, sure, you will be able to find a number students who want to train that way; but if you want to have a successful Black Belt Business, you are going to have to align your thinking more with your Target Market and less with the 1960s thinking of "Old School" Instructors.

4.3 So a drop in standards then?

No! It means **Higher Standards!**

For many students it will mean they get something other than 'warrior type training,' which would have meant they would have quit in week one. It will be substituted with a training programme which meets their own requirements and aspirations, built around their point of view.

Today, a much more sophisticated model of Martial Arts than the old days is required……..after all when was the last time you fought for your life?

The most common kind of attack nowadays is a Heart Attack! Surely if you can reduce the numbers of that type of attack you have done more good for Martial Arts than an Instructor who rejects students because they can't fight off ten men!

For the Warriors amongst you, you can always run Elite or Committed Martial Artist classes, where select students are drawn from the general population of the Black Belt Business. You can, and should, charge more for Elite classes; or you can charge less, or nothing at all for the select few if you like - it's your Business.

If you can only attract and retain 10 students, the chances of one of them becoming a 'Hard Core' student are slim to none. If you can attract and retain 500 students, the chances of a number of them becoming 'fully committed to the art' type of students are much higher.

In my experience, students don't start as hard core students anyway, they become hard core as they develop and grow. They want more knowledge and more challenges, and that's great - give it to them. Whether that's more Kata/Patterns, more Fighting, more Technical stuff, more Historical stuff, Street Fighting etc etc.

Remember, it is *your* Black Belt Business so you can have different approaches in different classes. Wouldn't it be nice to have a good financial income from a large number of students in a thriving school and an elite set of Master Students, whose excellence reflects your expectations?

You can have both as long as you can understand and meet the expectations of your target market.

4.4   Who is Your target market?

<u>**Pay Attention**</u> –

THIS is the most important sentence in the book!

<u>Your Target Market</u>

<u>IS NOT, Is Not, is not</u>

<u>IS NOT !</u>

<u>just Anyone who</u>

<u>wants to train!</u>

It is *not* just ANYONE who wants to train.

Because you can't appeal to everyone so don't try. Someone won't like you, whether it's children because you are too scary, or adults because you are too silly, or fit people because you don't run sweat sessions or older people because you do!

Your Black Belt Business needs to appeal most to the people who are going to be attracted to you because of what you do, how you do it, and the things that you stand for. These are the students who will stay with you for the longest, and will be happy to pay you again and again.

You probably have a good idea of the people you'd like to teach. That's a good starting point as long as it makes sense in light of the questions about the business you answered in Section 3. However, you may need to re-adjust your Target when you see the financial outcomes from concentrating on this group.

In this section I want to rank students into differing categories.

Category 'A' Students
Category 'B' Students
Category 'C' Students
Category 'D' Students

So what does a Category A Student look like?

These are the students who fit your Black Belt Business the best. They want what you have to offer, their values and beliefs probably align with yours and your business. They are ready, willing and able to pay to train with you. They are likely to have the same outlook on Martial Arts as you do. They like the discipline, the self-improvement, the energy level of what you do. They are the perfect fit for you. In short they are the people who are your biggest fans. They love it and you, and your business loves them. Their family is supportive of them and they will go out of their way to help you and your business become successful. They're 'Wow' students, not just in arm and leg waving, but in attitude and enthusiasm.

You could you do with a few hundred of them training every week.

Category B Students.

These are good reliable students who enjoy what you do. They are happy to support you and like what and how you teach. They are not the rabid fans of the Category A Student, but they are a good fit for your business. You would be happy to spend some time and energy on these people and they would be happy to receive it.

We like Category B Students – they're potential Category A's!

Category C Students

Ok, now things don't fit as well as with the other Category Students. These are not such good news for your Black Belt Business; they may not be good payers, they might want you to do more slow stuff when you want to go fast, they might resent the amount of time you spend with others and not with them - they are high maintenance and a bit of a pain. They don't share the values of your business, they hit other students, or don't hit other students when you want them to - in short, a bit of a pain in the rear. Not quite the wrong person in the wrong place, but something doesn't quite fit.

Category C Students might be able to be upgraded to Category B with some time, effort, and a bit more of an education into why you do what you do. Maybe. Good luck with those people.

Category D Students.

Unreliable, disinterested, unhelpful, 'why the hell did I let them through the door' students. Pain-in-the-arse students, not in physical ability, but in attitude.

Get Rid of Category D students. They are energy vampires and time wasters, and they bring you and everyone around them, down. Get rid of them - politely but quickly. Ensure you follow your values not theirs.

4.5 Most of your Customers Most of the Time

Hands up - who wants a business full of Category D Customers?

Thought not.

So the following pages will help you to clarify who you *do* want in your Black Belt Business, and, hence, identify your Target Market.

My Category A Students, and therefore the overwhelming majority of my new customers, will be....

Adult Men
Adult Women
16 to 24 year olds
Teenagers
8 to 12 year olds Boys/Girls
5 to 8 year olds Boys/Girls
Pre-school children Boys/Girls
Pensioners
Able-bodied/disabled
Physically Fit, Unfit, Average, Elite Athletes.

My Category A Students will be

....
....
....

And from which financial group? (Assists with setting charge rates, choosing locations, style of school, investment level.)

Unemployed

High income businessmen/women

Middle income

Lower income families

Aspirational parents

Pensioners

Retired high income

Arab Sheiks

Other group....if so, which?

I will target clients from the following financial group

....
....
....

This group will value or want (from lessons)

....
....
....
....

Continue to ask yourself questions, and, therefore, add to the profile of your Category A Student. The more clarity you have of who will love what you do, and about what you will love about them, the better. I can suggest some questions you might like to ask:

What are the biggest demographics in my locality right now?

Which demographic has the disposable income to pay for my lessons?

Am I targeting the best potential customers?

Who else might like to pay me to teach them?

Which sections of society do I want to draw from for students?

What is the biggest demographic (i.e. type of person) coming to my classes now

Which students stay the longest?

Who am I really good at teaching?

Who am I really attractive to? (No, not like that!)

Who will pay my hourly rate?

What would my ideal student look like? (For the best return for the business, not my ego).

Who would be in my ideal class? (Again, business).

Who **don't** you want to attract to your business?

Who **does not** fit in with your values?

Who will be more hassle than they are rewarding?

I am going to ask you to write, (or re-write), who and what your Category A Student is, and where they come from. Their background and values, and what they want from your classes. If you don't get it clear now, in a year or two's time when you have 300 Category C and D Students and your life is a TOTAL MISERY, don't blame me.

Come on write it out in as much detail as you can

My Target Market Category A Student is:-

Some who is

....
....
....
....
....
....
....
....
....

4.6 Add this to your vision

It should look something like this:-

I will create a Black Belt Business which will, in the next 2 years, generate an income of £50,000 per year through the teaching of abc students to become experts in Self Defence by utilising our xyz style of Karate.

And we will treat people as…..

                    if all can achieve success

And we will create feelings of….

                    Achievement, pride and self-worth etc

Our Black Belt Business Values…

        Honesty, clarity, perseverance, friendliness, strength, etc.

My Target Market Category "A" Students will be.

Children aged 5 to 8 years, with middle income aspirational parents from my town, who would look for a fun, friendly and safe environment, in which discipline, respect, self-development and self-confidence are highly valued.

Or

Male students aged 17 to 25, from working class tough areas, who want to become fighters, and who are prepared to give whatever is required to be the best and toughest competitors in England.

Yes I want you to write it all out again so it goes in, OK? ☺

I will Create a Black Belt Business which

……………………………………..……………..........................
………………………………………………………………………....
……………………………………………………………………….....
…………………………………………………………………………...
………………………………………………………………………..….
……………………………………………………………………….…..

We will treat our students as

…………………………………………………………………………...
…………………………………………………………………………...
………………………………………………………………………….....
…………………………………………………………………………...
…………………………………………………………………………...
…………………………………………………………………………...

We will create feelings of

…………………………………………………………..……………....
…………………………………………………………………………...
…………………………………………………………………………...
…………………………………………………………………………...
…………………………………………………………………………...
…………………………………………………………………………...

Our Business Values are

………………………………………………..……………………….
…………………………………………………………………………
…………………………………………………………………………
…………………………………………………………………………
…………………………………………………………………………

My Target Market, Category "A" Students are

....
....
....
....
....
....

Chapter 5   How will you teach what you teach?

5.1   Sorry, but *these* are really the most important sentences in this book!

When you are the Student,

it is Your Needs, Feelings

and Expectations

that Should be Met.

When you are the Instructor,

it is your Students' Needs,

Feelings and Expectations

that You need to Meet.

5.2 Paul McCartney

I know - you love Rough House, Ground and Pound, and you hate Aerobic Classes!

Sir Paul McCartney may well hate singing 'Hey Jude' - after all he's sung it a billion times, but his audience expect him to sing it, and if he doesn't they are less inclined to buy another ticket for the next gig. Then he gets the chance to sing some of his newer songs. He meets his audience's expectations, and then they go along with him.

So what will most of your classes be most of the time?

Once again, choosing the style of teaching (not the style of your Martial Art) is vitally important, and will lead your business to be attractive to a specific group or style of people who want to continue to pay to work with you.

What does your Target Market expect from an activity they choose? Because if you don't meet those expectations, they will go find another activity that does.

Not many will expect to go home damaged from their activity! Not many expect to be 'beasted' or verbally abused - even if it's in the interests of 'Self Defence'.

Remember, for a beginner, your life-long passion is just another activity for them to try!

So what would they value in a class?

What would they love to be doing?

What would make it a fantastic activity for them to take up?

What style of teacher would they look for?

The question is - can you hook them into your Martial Art? Can you gain a lifetime student….. or will they slip away?

If your Target Market is Mums, and your training style is gruelling, you may have to think again.

The **predominant** way your Target Market will want to train will be the way in which you should conduct the majority of your classes. (You can still have specialised classes which fall outside of the norm).

How can you make the classes engaging to your Target Market so they think it's the best thing they have ever done?

Have in mind your own personality, energy and expertise levels, together with your Target Market expectations, and, using answers like the ones below, give an answer to the following statements:

Calm , Methodical, Systematic, Dynamic, High energy, Fun

Exhausting, Pushing to the max, Traditional, Relaxing

Cardio based, Strength based, Scary, Disciplined, Crazy, Exciting, Aggressive.

I want my **Target Market** to feel **Fantastic** so my classes will primarily be

....
....
....
....
....

I know you want to add more. So go back and add additional objectives for your classes.

I still want my **Target Market** to feel **Fantastic** I am sure they would appreciate classes which are also have

....
....
....
....

So it might end up looking something like this

My Students will feel Fantastic because the classes are primarily high energy fun, and because they learned something new, and where they were made to feel great in every lesson. Or it might be,

My students will feel fantastic because they've worked their hearts out to the max and achieved new heights of endurance and strength. Every time they train, they Feel are becoming invincible.

5.3 Now Add this to your Vision Statement

Same again.... (You didn't learn a round house kick by just doing it two or three times, now did you? Come on you should know it by now anyway).

I will Create a Black Belt Business which
....
....
....
....
....
....

We will treat our students as
....
....
....
....
....
....

We will create feelings of
....
....
....
....
....

Our Business Values are

....
....
....
....
....

My Target Market, Category "A" Students are

....
....
....
....
....

My Students will feel Fantastic because the classes are

....
....
....
....
....
....

Chapter 6   Does it make sense to you?

6.1   Just a Quick Check

Ok - it's time just to do a quick check. Does what we have written make any Business sense?

Have a look at the answers you have given and see if they do; not just to you, but to a NON-Martial Artist's Point of View if possible.

Are the answers congruent?

If your answers are

Section 3.2	(Money)	Replace salary of £50,000
Section 3.3	(Objectives)	Street Fighters
Section 4.4	(Who)	5 to 8 years olds
Section 5.2	(Class Style)	Fun

In my opinion this is crazy. Finding enough 5 to 8 year olds, whose parents would allow you to train them as street fighters in order for you to earn £50k is a long shot - even if the classes *were* fun. (And they probably wouldn't be).

If you were to sacrifice the Street Fighter answer in exchange for creating 'greater confidence', then you may achieve a much better result.

6.2 Will your answers give you what you want from your business?

If the answers to the above sections are as follows:

Section 3.2   To have a good level of income

Section 3.3   Technical Experts

Section 4.4   Families and the unemployed

Section 5.2   Serious

Then the likely outcome is that you will have difficulty creating a 'rapid growth school' with a good financial outcome.

You are unlikely to be able to make a satisfactory level of income if you have identified that your core students are from the ranks of the unemployed. Not impossible, as there may be grants and other business formats (Charitable Status etc.), that might enable it to work. But at first glance it seems that the answers above would mean your business model would be similar to setting yourself up for an uphill swim.

In order to have a rapid growth school the answers to the above must be congruent, or at the very least sympathetic to each other.

What if your answers look like the set below?

Section 3.2   Teaching to pay for your own training
Section 3.3   General improvement in fitness
Section 4.4   Pensioners
Section 5.2   Easy Going

This combination may very well work as a series of answers; however, as the main objective, (Section 3:1), is so low, it may only be a realistic business if you just want to 'give back'.

6.3   Your Answers, Your Business!

So you now have four answers, one from each of the above sections. The next thing is to honestly examine what outcome, in business terms, these answers will likely result in.

Are they congruent with running a Black Belt Business which provides the income level you require?

Is your product, (what you do and how you offer it), appealing enough to your Target Market? Will you reach enough people that can afford your it, in order to enable you to run your business in the manner you describe, and obtain the financial rewards you want?

If not, then you must adjust what you do and how you do it, or find another Target Market.

6.4 Actually, I think *this* really is the most important sentence in this book.

Your Income

is a Direct Result of

your Customers being Delighted

with what you do,

time after time

after time,

after time,

after time

after time!

Will your Black Belt Business achieve the financial expectations you want, when answering the above question?

Does the 'Product', "the offer" appeal sufficiently to the people to whom you are trying to sell it, and can they afford it? Will they be delighted with the product?

If it doesn't, and they aren't, then you need to think again.

6.5 Just for reference.

If I was to answer the questions with regard to writing this book, my answers would be:

Section 3.2   To provide extra income for the nice things. (Just like J K Rowling.)

Section 3.3   To provide excellent Martial Arts Specific Business information.

Section 4.4   In a straightforward, light and easy-going style.

Section 5.2   To experienced Martial Artists planning to start a club, who will see the information as valuable, and who can afford the cover price.

I hope at this point you can see that the logic of my earnings ambition is realistic, when answering the question:

Does the content and style of the book appeal to the people I am selling it to and can they afford the investment?

Answer:-

Well you bought it. I am honoured that you did and trust it is of value to you. Thank you.

6.6 DO THIS!

PLEASE

DO THIS NEXT SECTION

In this section I give you a couple of differing Vision and Mission Statements. Have a look at them and see how they encompass the feelings of two very different Black Belt Businesses.

Example 1   My Vision is to

Create a Black Belt Business which will, in the next 2 years, generate an income of £50,000 per year through the teaching of teenage students to become experts in Self Defence by utilising our combat style of Karate.

Example 1   My Mission is to

Create a business where people love to come and train because they will be treated with kindness and courtesy. They will learn and progress in a friendly, welcoming environment.

We will be honest and open in order to help people progress and feel a pride in themselves through their achievement.

The classes will be high energy and develop the students physically as well as transferring knowledge.

We have a passion for improving people's lives and it will show in everything we do.

Example 2   My Vision is to:-

Create a Black Belt Business which will, in the next 2 years, generate an income of £50,000 per year through the teaching of students to become the best Sport Fighters in England.

Example 2   My Mission is to:-

Provide an environment where the elite fighters train with the best facilities in the country.

We will only accept excellence and 100% commitment to becoming the best. Our training will be harsh and brutal. We expect every drop of energy from our students.

The environment will run with competitiveness; 2nd place is the 1st of the losers! We will be the best!

6.7 The Mission Statement for Team Black Belt

I have included my Mission Statement below, (not because it is right or wrong – it happens to be right for me and my Black Belt Business), but it might give you ideas of what to include in yours. (Or not!)

I have not included the first part, ('The Vision'), as it's *my* vision and *my* financial wishes…. Get your own!!!

Team Black Belt Mission

We will positively affect the lives of children, both physically and mentally, by raising their self-esteem and inspiring their self-confidence to enable them to soar.

We will Support Boost, Champion, Encourage, Motivate and Inspire others to reach their potential.

We will achieve this by engaging with them through Martial Arts Activities and the use of Personal Safety Programmes, Life Skills and Personal Development tools.

We will create a Warm, Safe Positive and Professional Environment and Business.

In the above Mission there is no mention of Black Belts or Competitions or Karate Standards. We have all of those in our business, but to me they are a by-product of doing the above.

So you see, although I am writing about a Black Belt Business making money, all I want to do is to Give Back, to make others feel as good as I did the day I passed my Black Belt. I think my Mission has a value to children and the parents of those children, (much more of a value than a TV Sports Subscription), and I can't do it if I'm living in a cardboard box.

This bit, is the bit to DO!

Now go back and have a look at YOUR Vision Statement.

Now check it makes sense to you. Then give it to your Mum and see what she thinks, give it to your significant other, in fact give it to any NON Martial Artist and ask them if it makes sense.

Re-write it if necessary, so that it makes sense, and anyone who sees it will understand what you are about to do with your Black Belt Business.

Your Vision   What you want!

Your Mission   How you do what is needed to achieve your Vision, and what you and your Business stand for.

Get Clear on the reasons you are going to do what you are going to do. Why are you doing this as opposed to starting a hamburger stall, or a flower shop?

If you have done your Vision and Mission I congratulate you. But not as much as you will congratulate yourself when the success you have defined here starts to materialise. You have made clear decisions about yourself and your business, and when choices arise you have a reference point you can go back to and check which option matches your business vision and mission.

You need to understand that taking an additional training fee from a person who does not align with your Vision or Mission Values may give you an extra £30 a month income, but will cost you much more in the long run.

Teaching a 'battle hard' lesson to a group of your Target Market Mums may make YOU feel good, but it will damage your Black Belt Business, so stay aligned to your business and its values.

The people who join a group, club, Martial Art club etc, do so because they expect to get what THEY want from the activity. They will align their values with a group which shares the same values. If you don't know what your values are, or what you stand for, then you are at best a confusing proposition for new members, and at worst someone who just wants to take the money. People are too sharp to fall for that.

If you haven't joined in and written your Vision and Mission by now, you probably won't, and reading the rest of this book will be a waste of your time. So do me and all those people out there who so desperately need what Martial Arts has to offer a favour, pass this book onto an instructor who will.

Or you could……

GO BACK AND DO IT NOW!

Chapter 7   LOCATION, Location, Location

7.1   Location, Location, Location

It doesn't matter if you are looking for a single facility or multiple locations; a few simple concepts are important. The first is, of course, the general location, the second is the specific location and the third is the micro location.

7.2   LOCATION

General Location - the Geographical Area

Where is your Target Market? Where does your Target Market live, work or commute through?

When considering the location, it is important to view the demographics of the surrounding area. What is the area like?

Affluent middle class with children and disposable incomes maybe, or on its last legs - an estate without a penny to spare? A small village with 700 occupants, a large town with 250,000 people, or a district within a large city?

Is the area concerned affluent and growing, or has the last job just been taken out of the place?

As the local demographics will dictate the likely returns on your investment, you need to do your homework.

The larger chains of health clubs have done a lot of this work for you. They all look for aspirational families with disposable income, and are unlikely to have invested millions in a gym in an area with no population who could afford to join it. (Unlikely but not unheard of.)

So take a drive around, get a feel for the area. Is there enough of your Target Market around to make the investment of your money, time and energy worthwhile?

The more schools, health clubs, offices, factories or large supermarkets there are, who are catering for the type of customer you want, (as outlined by your answer to question 4 in your Mission Statement), the better.

So the demographics of an area where you want to open your Dojo, are vitally important to your success in the Black Belt Business.

Do your homework. Many Martial Arts clubs open where they can get premises, not where the best locations are. The best locations may take more effort and time to acquire, but remember, the better the general location, the more of your Target Market will be available, the more likely it will be that your Black Belt Business will make you a decent income.

So, time to write down a few ideas of 'ideal locations' for your Dojo:

....
....
....
....
....
....
....
....

7.3 Location 2

Specific Location – the Venue

What type of premises do you want to teach in?

I have seen, first-hand, many Martial Arts schools which are located in school halls, church halls, the room at the back of a doggy pub, in fact the first available building that has come along; at the back of somewhere, down a drive, with little or no parking, in a rough area, with poor/ non-existent lighting.

Who wants to walk 400 meters in the rain across a poorly lit piece of waste ground next to the roughest pub in the city? What Mum in her right mind would bring her children to your class?

If your Mum wouldn't come, you can't expect anyone else to, and it's not the right location for your Black Belt Business.

It will cost more to have the right premises, maybe double or treble the cost of the worst places, but there's a reason for that. The right venues know they attract the right people; and the poorer, rougher venues can't get people through the door, and so they charge less.

You are going to make money based upon the number of students who come to your classes and pay you. It doesn't matter how cheap the place is to rent, if no-one turns up, it still costs you money. If you can rent the local sports centre with thousands of people visiting the place to do sports activities it must be better than a local hovel, which everyone avoids.

A key consideration with your venue is whether the classes are visible from the outside by the general public? Not so they can peer in and gawp, but so they can see a Martial Arts class in progress from the street? If so, your marketing expenditure is reduced so you can pay more for the venue! Can the public see signage from the street and will your venue allow the signage to be displayed? Again, this will reduce your marketing expenditure.

Obtain the best premises you can get. As a new, potentially long term renter, you could be a valuable client to the landlord, and you may be in a strong position to have a number of weeks free or at a reduced rent until you build up your Black Belt Business. Ask them to work with you. It is in the landlord's interest to have good, stable, long term clients; and after all, you are doing a worthy job, helping the community, keeping kids off the streets and teaching respect and discipline.

Remember, rent a venue that your Mum would be proud to know you are teaching in.

7.4 Your own Venue

I am not at this point going to go through the benefits and pitfalls of venue ownership. Suffice to say that there are many advantages in having your own venue, whether leased, mortgaged or owned, but there are also some down-sides.

A single location may not have the amount of people living close enough to make it viable, the costs per teaching hour may well be higher than renting (if you lease, you lease it for 168 hours a week!). If you only want to teach for 20 hours a week… well you do the maths. Factor in premises maintenance and up-keep, rates, utilities etc…. I know, I've got a full time Dojo.

However, the benefits of having a full time Dojo are fantastic though. The room is always available if I need it, I never have to work around anyone else's timetable or commitments - basically it's available whenever I want it, and is exactly what I want it to be inside and out.

In general, all the same rules apply; the better the facilities, the more attractive the place, the happier people are to attend.

So what are the key elements your venue must have? Go on write them down. (I know Nag, Nag!)

....
....
....
....
....
....
....

7.5   Location 3

Micro Location - the Training Environment.

I appreciate that some of the greatest boxers ever have come from crappy little sweat box gyms; however some of the best trainers make little or no money from their gyms, and are rewarded occasionally on a percentage of purse basis. In Martial Arts that's a fairly precarious business model!

You will most likely build your Black Belt Business and income through the attraction and retention of students. The environment in which they train must be congruent with their point of view, so you must make the effort to transform the room into a Marital Arts venue that they feel good about.

The training area should be brightly lit, welcoming, impressive not scary and matted (or at least mats should be available). Your Philosophy, Mission Statement and Code of Conduct should all be in view.

Hanging banners around the school gym will go a long way towards the job of transforming a school gym or hall into a Martial Arts studio.

Are there changing facilities and toilets? Even these basics I have seen ignored by some excellent Martial Arts Masters. (They only had 6 students though).

If you are going to have a successful Black Belt Business then you must see your business through the eyes of an outsider; would your Mum like it here? What would she think? The message must be that you welcome students to your venue and you care about their needs, aspirations and points of view.

My venue will make people think that we are

....
....
....
....
....
....
....

and will create the impression of

....
....
....
....
....
....
....

By using

....
....
....
....
....
....
....
....

7.6 Equipment

You will doubtless need some equipment for your teaching. Remember students today expect more than an empty hall to run around in - they are used to visiting well equipped gyms. Equipment can differentiate your Black Belt Business from the rest. Do you have a matted area so students are safe? Do you utilise punch bags and striking equipment? If you do, you can charge more; it shows you are professional and have invested in your business.

Would you book a DJ to do a party only to find he has no lighting, rubbish speakers or, worse, no music to play? Not much of a DJ eh? He would give you a poor experience, and you certainly wouldn't book him twice would you?

It would be ridiculous to hire a DJ who didn't have the right kit, yet many Black Belt Businesses don't have even the basics. If you don't even have Focus pads, something to motivate people and to provide variety in training, you appear just as amateur as the DJ with no sounds. It's time to invest.

I recommended to a friend and fellow instructor, that he buy a free-standing kick bag for his junior students to strike against, which he subsequently purchased with some degree of reluctance. Within a week he had gained 5 new students from referrals made by his existing students telling their mates what a great time they had had punching and kicking this new bit of kit. His investment in the kick bag was recouped within its first week, and he gained five new sets of fees, sorry, I mean students.

The equipment can pay for itself by gaining referrals and boosting retention levels; don't skimp here.

Chapter 8   Show me the Money

8.1   Important Sentences.

<u>You are going to Give More Value, to More People, than most will ever give and you will Change Lives for the Better.</u>

So be Proud of your Profession and be a Professional Instructor and Business Owner.

8.2 What's a lesson worth?

£8.72 per lesson (35 or 45 minutes long)

Well, that's my charge rate at the moment - April 2012.

I have over 300 students and a 4 to 9 month waiting list for some classes.

When the school 500 yards away is charging £2.50 for a two hour lesson and they have very few students, I must be the greatest Martial Artist since Bruce Lee right....? Wrong. I am an average Martial Artist, but a very good Instructor who has got things right (touch wood). The school down the road must be rubbish, right....? Wrong. They teach some great stuff, they are very good Martial Artists.

You see, what a lesson is worth is dependent on lots of factors.

Your General, Specific and Micro locations play a significant part in what you are able to charge, but charges for lessons can also differ according to all kinds of other factors.

For example, the added value of:

Classes at peak times of the day or week,

Private or size limited classes.

Life skills programmes.

Black belt classes, Master level programmes.

Train the trainer/ Leadership programmes.

Elite programmes.

Sometimes I charge LESS. On many occasions I waive higher fees for assistance with the school. A simple trade off and something you can use if you want - it's your business.

Maybe you'd like to offer free lessons or discounted rates to disadvantaged students, or certain special free added value programmes?

Of course you would, you're a Martial Artist and you have a generous side! But keep it in check, and plan your charitable donations to students in the same way as you plan your business success.

Plan it in your budget... there I said it - the B word - BUDGET.

8.3   Show me the Money

It's your Black Belt Business so suit yourself. The hours you work will, to some degree, dictate the income you receive. Should you wish to teach for two evenings a week for no more than two hours, fine. If you can identify and attract a sufficient number of students who are willing to pay the kind of fees which give you the lifestyle you want, go for it.

Should you want to have a strong, successful, lucrative Black Belt Business, you may have to be prepared to work longer hours.

When I first started my Black Belt Business I was told by someone for whom I had a great deal of respect (and still do) that attracting students on Friday evenings was very difficult, and Saturday evenings was impossible so I didn't open then.

I have a strong, successful Black Belt Business and so far, we have never opened on a Friday night. However, in the course of the last few years, I have met many owners of Black Belt Businesses who didn't receive the same advice as me and they run massive Friday and Saturday evening classes.

It is my belief that if your product is sufficiently appealing to your Target Market, they will come on any evening that you open.

I don't run regular Saturday or Sunday morning classes, and this may well be a major mistake, but I have 300 students training Monday to Thursday. I know of highly successful Black Belt Businesses which run weekends only.

Again, your business, you choice. Be aware of your Target Market and their availability patterns.

You could, should you choose, work 24 hours a day, seven days a week running classes for various target groups: Mums in the morning, pensioners in the afternoon, kids early evening, adults till late at night, 2.30am classes for shift workers, professional courses for corporate clients all day long etc. etc.

So, should you work yourself to death and then fall out of love with your Martial Art because, within a few months of starting your Black Belt Business, it's just become a pain-in-the-behind slog of a job?

Well, I hope not. I hope I can help.

If you need to have an income of £25,000 per annum and you ideally would like to teach for 10 hours a week for 46 weeks of the year, the sums are easy:

£25,000 divided by 46 weeks equals £543.48p each week you work.

Divide that by 10 hours a week and you need to have a net income of £54.35 per hour.

Or 11 students per hour, each paying £5
11 students per hour x 10 hours teaching each week = £25k

(22 students per hour x 10 hours teaching each week = £50k!)

Or, how about 3 nights and a Saturday morning, for 4 hours' or 4 lessons each day, with 20 students paying £5 per hour's lesson?

16 hours x 20 students x £5 x 46 weeks = £73,600 per year.

Or at £7.50 per session, that would come to £110,400 per year for working 16 hours a week – just 1 instructor!

For doing what you love to do….. and to be able to excel at it.

Are you 'selling out' for providing excellence in your field, for giving back to your students the feelings you got when you passed your Black Belt just because you don't do it on the cheap? Of course not. You will become more expert, more proficient, more dedicated.

Believe me, you are going to give More Value, to More People, than most will ever Give and you will Change Lives for the Better.

So be Proud of your Profession and be a *Professional* Instructor and Business Owner.

8.4 The Real Reason for charging more:

Know what you are Selling.

It is most important to know what you are selling. When I started my professional career in Martial Arts, a friend of mine asked me and I quote "What did you get out of martial arts?"

I struggled for a minute, and then he asked me "What feelings did doing Martial Arts give you, what feelings did you have on the day you passed your Black Belt?"

Ah….the penny dropped. Not confident, way past confident; not strong, way past strong. I felt…..indestructible. I felt like I could fly. Superman. Unstoppable. A force of nature…..

Then he asked me "How much money was that worth… how much money would I have to give you in order to take back those feeling so you never had them?"

The answer is that there is no amount of money that you could give me in order to take back those feelings. No amount.

So you see, I don't sell waving your arms and legs about, I sell Feeling Fantastic; Gaining Confidence; Becoming Healthy; Being Able to look after yourself. I sell Inspiration and Positive Values in a world of depressing news, poor role models and a lack of leadership.

For me to teach a student and to facilitate them having those feelings, I charge £9 a lesson.

8.5   What are your Martial Arts lessons worth?

If you sell your lessons cheaply and compete on price with other activities, such as the club down the road or the local keep fit class, you are selling all Martial Arts short.

What we do, know and teach is highly valued in society. Please, for your sake and every other Martial Artist, don't give it away.

As a Martial Artist you are one of the few people who live by a set of values, with the ability to become a leader of others. Leaders with high moral standards and influence over others are rare and valued.

Charge for the value you give, and not just how much learning to punch is worth.

How much is a Martial Arts Lesson worth in the days when Fish and Chips costs £6 and TV Sports package is £40, Gym Memberships are £75 and more; to get a computer fixed will cost you £75 to start with and my garage door cost me £105 to replace two lift wires…?

So Give Value and be Expensive, Because, as they say in the ads, 'You're worth it!'

I know that you are sceptical that you can charge what you really want to charge, so to make it easy, to start with you can start lower and increase the fees over time. So complete the following.

To start with I will charge £………. per lesson

and then raise lessons to £…….. per lesson by …………..

But there are a few other considerations to make, so we will go on to look at them, you may come back and change the figures you have just written down!

8.6   Fee structures

You have worked out your price per class. Hopefully it scares you to charge it. It will make you try harder to give the correct level of training/value for money.

Don't worry, no-one knows the price of your type of Martial Arts lesson except you.

If you were going to buy a car you could spend £500 and it would get you from A to B. Or you could buy a car which costs £250,000 which does the same job.

Ok in a bit more style I grant you, but £249,500 dearer than the other car?

People do buy cars at £250,000 and then they go on a waiting list so it becomes an object of desire.

If you charge £5, £7.50, £10 a lesson it's only you that's struggling with the amount. The people who want what you are offering will happily pay for it (your Target Market).

8.7 How many lessons a week should your students attend?

Well, that's up to you. Once a week is enough for many students, certainly for juniors, or for the first year or two of training.

Maybe twice a week for adults, but remember the more times a week they train the more discount you will be expected to give and there is only so many teaching hours available.

A 'Student Teaching Hour' is a 'Student Teaching Hour', 3 Students paying £5 per hour is £15.

Why should 1 Student who trains for 3 hours get it for £10?

A Student Teaching Hour is worth a £x value whether it is 1 student or 3 students.

I would recommend allowing students to train more than once a week by invitation only. That way you can choose the students with the right stuff to have the 'honour' of training with you. You can also keep the charge rate high as it is a privileged position. No need to offer discounts at all.

If you have limited resources you may not want any '2 or 3 times per week' students. If you have a limited class capacity, for whatever reason, offering discounts to those who want to take up a space on another evening is just cutting your own throat. Don't offer a discount.

If you want to encourage students to train 2 or 3 times a week you might consider a discount structure but ensure that you calculate your fees backwards from your 'Student Teaching Hour'. For example, how much money do you want for teaching a student 3 times a week, for an hour at a time, i.e. 3 Student Teaching Hours?

If you decide a student hour is £5, then perhaps the starting point should be a charge of £6 per student for a single lesson (or more) if you want them to attend twice a week plus.

A student who trains twice a week could be offered a discount so the charge is not 2x the single hour rate, (i.e. £12), but £11 per week; and a student who trains 3 times gets the full discount, so is charged £15 per week instead of £18.

Students will very quickly work out that attending and paying for 3 lessons a week is much better value and your Black Belt Business will be busy collecting the correct Student Teaching Hourly Rate.

8.8 Additional family member Discounts?

Additional family members. This is a bit of a dilemma, as they take up just as much teaching time as non-related students, however they expect a discounted rate! (So keep your Student Teaching Hourly Rate in mind.) It is my belief that a discounted rate should show an element of goodwill rather than be a substantial amount of money. Should one family member recommend your teaching to another family member, they know the benefits of your business and should expect to pay for them.

As a suggestion, a discount to round down the figures to a sensible number is a good idea, or a maximum discount of 10% for each new family member. Generally, it seems that Martial Arts Instructors undervalue themselves and give away too much in discounts.

It's your Black Belt Business, so you can charge and discount as you please, even allowing students to train for free is ok. Put it in your budget, record it and measure it.

8.9 Pay as You Go or Monthly Collection?

Have you ever run out of money at the end of the month? Have you ever missed training through illness? Have you missed training because of the England (insert your own team here) Match? Have you ever missed training because of a family issue? Have you ever just been too tired to go?

Well, on that day, the day that you didn't pay him, your Instructor turned up to teach you and the room he hired still had to be paid for. He didn't get a replacement student for the night - his income was reduced.

You don't want your income to be reduced, do you?

MONTHLY, MONTHLY, MONTHLY, MONTHLY!

Get your students to pay for their PLACE in your Black Belt Business, not whether they turn up or not. As you are kind hearted, you can always allow a missed lesson to be made up on another night.

It's a no-brainer: get a direct debit collection service and collect your money every month from your students - no hassle.

I work with Gerard from Nest Management, a specialist Martial Arts direct debit collection service and I have done so since the day I set up my Black Belt Business. They do a great job for me collecting fees but their wealth of knowledge (and their willingness to share it) born through working with thousands of Black Belt Businesses, is invaluable. If that sounds like a plug for them, and I sound like a fan of these guys, It is and I am. www.nestmanagement.co.uk

It's easy and reliable, and your student doesn't have to think about money, it's all sorted. They just turn up and train.

Any collection service will cost you, but it's not as much as you will lose in non-attendance on a pay-as-you-go mat fee.

Should you not want to use the services of a direct debit collection company, standing order mandate forms can be obtained from most high street banks and modified with your details, so a new student can complete with their bank details for you to take to your bank.

The downside of that route, however, is should you want to increase or alter the tuition fee, (and students also often request a leave of absence, change the number of times they train each week, change their bank account etc), you will need new a standing order form to be completed by the student, and that is a pain. Still, it's much better than pay as you go!

My advice, Check out Nest.

8.9   These are the most important sentences in the book!

I will NOT accept

Pay-as-you-Go

Students...Ever.

I will charge my students for their place in my class, not whether they attend or not and I will use a Direct Debit Collection Service or Standing Orders.

Chapter 9   Keeping it a Secret!

9.1   Yes more important sentences!

If you are not

Actively Marketing

your Black Belt Business

then you are *Actively*

keeping it a Secret!

9.2 Get Clear

Before you market your Black Belt Business you need to be very clear about your TARGET MARKET. I said you would need to know it and I repeat it now. You have completed this in section 4.4 - please write it out again.

My main customers will be

....
....
....
....
....

From the financial group

....
....
....
....
....

My target market would love to have what?
....
....
....
....
....

My Target market would think my lessons are fantastic if they
……………………………………………………………
……………………………………………………………
……………………………………………………………
……………………………………………………………
……………………………………………………………

The stand out thing which appeals to my target market is
……………………………………………………………
……………………………………………………………
……………………………………………………………
……………………………………………………………
……………………………………………………………

But now we have to add to it. What would you need to say, do, show and be, in order attract these people to your Black Belt Business (as opposed to the school down the road)?

Is the target market you want as students different to those whom you want to attract in marketing terms? If that sounds a little bizarre, consider that Team Black Belt's Target Market is 7 year old boys; they are who we want to have as starters in our classes. The Target Market for advertising purposes is the *mothers* of seven year old boys. Clearly a different marketing strategy is involved. (Less 'Kerpow' and more 'we care about your children').

So what would your Target Market be attracted to? What would motivate them to want to join your Black Belt Business?

If I look at typical Martial Arts advertising and promotion I see high kicks, breaking boards, big muscles, 'turn yourself into a killing machine' people depicted punching away attackers. All of which may look good to other Martial Artists, but to *your* Target Market? Really?

In my opinion what most people want is to know they will have a great time, and that it will be fun, bright, engaging, safe and welcoming. They will learn a useful skill, gain in confidence, get fitter, de-stress or enjoy personal development.

If you are hard core, that's fine, but think what message you are sending to people who see your marketing. 'Come to me and I will kick the living daylights out of you' might not be the best way to attract prospective students.........

So, in addition to the Target Market questions you answered, please answer the following:

What does my target market value most in life?
....
....
....
....

What qualities do they look for in an activity (or their child's activity)?
....
....
....
....

What outcomes would they like to achieve?
....
....
....
....

What would make them want to come and see us? The promise of what?
....
....
....
....

If they do this then they get what?

....
....
....
....

9.3 They Ain't Bothered

In my experience very few 'non-Martial Artists' know, or are interested in the founder in Japan, China or anywhere else. Which style is which, or which Association is headed by whom. Very few want to break things or to become indestructible.

Why then is the Martial Arts Industry obsessed with these details? The answer may be that they are very important to Martial Artists as a source of identity, a validation of our dedication, and belief in the system we have chosen, (by accident mainly); but to a new punter they are irrelevant.

As irrelevant as how the flow of electrons around a circuit board is to someone who just presses a remote control to turn the television over.

THEY AIN'T BOTHERED.

THEY *AIN'T* BOTHERED how many championships you have won, how many Dans you are, who you were photographed with in 1983.

THEY AIN'T BOTHERED.

THEY want what **THEY** want. And **THEY** are asking you "What's in it for **ME**?"

Many Martial Arts Clubs scare off potential students due to the instructors 'Martial Arts Mind'. What impresses a seasoned Martial Artist can be very different from what impresses a new, potential student.

The typical picture on a leaflet of a young child kicking an adult in the groin in a self-defence situation may be intended to say to a potential student "look how this child can defend himself" but may in fact translate to a non-Martial Artist Mum as, "we teach children to be violent towards others". Another student you will never have!

Club Logos - don't get me started on club logos. Japanese, Chinese, Korean symbols; Fists, Dragons, Fighting Emblems - in fact anything so it looks as if your badge might be for the membership of a cross between a Hells Angel gang and a Somali pirate outfit.

For heaven's sake don't show that what you do might be enjoyable fun or interesting! No, just scare everyone away, why don't you, with your skull and cross-bones logo!

Your Black Belt Business will grow by being ATTRACTIVE to potential students by matching their Values, Wants and Needs.

And next, the most important sentence in this book.

They 'Ain't Bothered' about you or your past.

They Want, what They Want and are asking You

"What's in it for Me?"

Market to Their Wants Not Yours!

Please complete the following:

The Key benefits for a student coming to my Black Belt Business are

....
....
....
....
....
....

The main message in my marketing will be

....
....
....
....
....
....

My Target Market will love this because

....
....
....
....
....
....

9.4 Your Identity

How are you going to present yourself to the outside world? How are you going to get the messages that you wish to send to your Target Market across to them - that your Black Belt Business is the place to go for great fun, fitness, traditional martial art or modern freestyle stuff set to music?

I use the word 'brand' but it's more of an image to explain to your Target Market in an instant what you do and the style in which you do it.

So what is your brand? What's your logo going to look like? What, if any, is your strap line or key message? What font style are you going to use? How many, and which, colours are you going to have?

Again, I want to challenge the established images I see Martial Artists use. Remember, you are not trying to impress other Martial Artists; you are trying to be as attractive as possible to your Target Market. So if your target market is women over 50 years old, look at other businesses that are trying to attract these women (especially the ones who are getting it right). If it's children, watch children's TV and get an idea of what the advertisers are doing to sell to children, and the parents of children.

Pictures of you or people performing flying kicks, smashing bricks etc. are very 'old school'. Promoting self-defence by showing kids kicking a bloke in the groin may be an empowering image for a youngster, and I understand the message you are trying to convey, but the same image may send out the wrong message to the parent who wants his/her son/daughter to be able to look after him/herself, but not in such an overtly violent manner.

Traditional oriental characters give the traditional message but mean very little to Western eyes. Association lettering you know: EKTN, WTTFF, JKFE, XYZ mean nothing to anyone outside the organisation, and your target market are exactly that - OUTSIDE.

So give your Logo wording and key message some serious thought. Rebranding afterwards can be expensive, time consuming and upsetting to existing students who have bought into the first brand.

9.5 Have a credible website

Long, long ago in a place far far away, there wasn't the internet - and then there was. And some people didn't embrace it. (I was one of them but that's another embarrassing story.) Now, if you don't have a web presence, you are out of the game.

The cost of a credible website is a few hundred pounds - I can put you in touch with designers if required - and the cost of NOT having a credible website is thousands and thousands of pounds.

A good credible site is what is required. You are not IBM, Marks and Spencer, or Wal-Mart so it doesn't have to be so slick you slide off your seat looking at it; simplicity is the key. It needs to be functional, with the required information presented in a manner which will appeal to your Target Market.

NO flashing banners, NO crazy graphics, NO pumping sound tracks and other web designer rubbish (they want the site to be the attraction - you want the Message to be the attraction!).

In researching this book, I viewed hundreds of websites, many of which I wish I hadn't seen. My old eyes and ears hurt. Make it easy to receive your message; don't try to blast it into the viewer's head!

A few sites with a Come along NOW! / Sign up NOW! / Do it NOW! approach may have some value. I personally think that being a bit more respectful and helpful may portray your image as more open and professional; a warmer person to be involved with. But hey it's your Black Belt Business - it's your call.

Remember: 'What's in it for me?' That's what the viewer of your site is asking. The site should answer that first, then the logistics, (the how where and when) should be easy to find; how they make contact, what is the next thing they have to do - ring, e-mail or just turn up etc?

Your key message or a few key messages - the ones that will motivate your Target Market to the next stage - should pervade the site.

I suggest you have a look at the thousands of examples of Martial Arts web sites and compare them with sites for fitness clubs, dance groups and take your pick. Copy the best bits, leave the nasty.

9.6 If a picture says a thousand words, a video might say a million.

Pictures on your website are fantastic if used correctly. Remember, you can show the prospective student 'what's in it for them'. It showcases the environment, the style, (way you are), and the other students getting the things they want to get and the feelings they want to feel.

Videos do it even better. In my opinion, there is no need for HD glamour and extensive production which can make the clip slow to download (irritating the viewer) and, if too produced, give a 'this is fake' effect to the viewer, who then starts to doubt what they are seeing.

Show them genuine students, the ones who are just like them, 'strugglers', people who are not too expert, beginners who have started to 'get it'. It shows what they can expect to achieve in a reasonable amount of time, not you and 30 years' of training performing your signature double-spinning-over-the-back-thrusting-death kick.

9.7 Testimonials

Social proof; others saying good things about you and your Black Belt Business can't do any harm. Any nice stories or anecdotes help make the Business more personal sounding and therefore accessible to the viewer, and in this day and age, everyone automatically looks for 'reviews' of everything. In video format it is even better.

9.8 About Us (yawn)

Yes, you need some information 'About Us'. It is a reasonable page for your site, however it is for the viewer's interest, not an opportunity for your ego to run away with itself. A reasonable amount of information, why you teach what you teach, how you teach it and the aims of your Black Belt Business. You definitely don't need to create a catalogue of every competition you have been placed in, or your life story. Remember 'What's in it for me?' is the question in the viewer's mind, and at the stage where they are ready to look at the About Us page they just need some reassurance that you are qualified to teach them and are a legitimate business - not a psycho-lunatic.

This is your opportunity to answer some of the unasked questions to reassure them that they are making the right decision in taking the next step. To reaffirm that you are the right Instructor for them, the one who understands their needs and desires as the Target Market and that you are the Black Belt Business for them.

9.9   Website Rankings

The higher the Google ranking, the more chance there is of your website being viewed.

I get my site to the top of the Google search page by means of ad words, the paid for position provided by Google. It works fantastically for me, and I live in a smaller Google area so I pay for that area only. It may be expensive for those living in a large Google area, but you can be selective as to which 'Search words' you pay for, and you can cap the daily expenditure. For me, it's great.

There are alternatives to push your 'non-paid for' rankings higher, some involving mysterious things called meta tags and other such things 'programmed in to your site' - techy stuff.

The more interaction on your site the higher it is likely to go; diaries, events, videos, and social media inputs all help. Blogs and links to other sites also do your rankings no harm.

You may have guessed, I am not in the slightest bit techy, (I would still use pigeons for mail if I could), however many Martial Arts students I have found are fantastic at this stuff, so if you know the right people, it can be very inexpensive to get your site up the rankings.

9.10 Social Media - DO IT!

Do It. Do it. Do it. It's FREE - what are you waiting for? Access to thousands of people in your area, all linked to each other, all sharing what a great Black Belt Business is running down the road. Ok, it might take a bit of building, but get on with it. Facebook, Google+, and Twitter at the time of writing are the most popular, with Facebook approaching 1 Billion users. The social media providers may change at any time but for now they are what I recommend. LinkedIn and Pinterest are up and coming - have a look. Social media is not going away any time soon. Create a page or account for your Black Belt Business and start to get the word out.

9.11 YouTube

As with social media sites, YouTube is FREE (at the time of writing!). Create a video of your Class (2 to 3 min clip) showcasing your most attractive features to your Target Market. Phones with a video camera are everywhere. What would have taken a film crew and recording studio to produce at enormous cost just a few years ago, can be done for next to nothing today. Take advantage of it, film and post to YouTube a promotional video, remember to select the 'Key words' on YouTube so the video can be found by people in your area. YouTube is second only to Google for searches, make sure you are found by your Target Market.

(Contact details at the start and end of the video, of course!)

Tie the videos in, and publicise them each week, with your social media campaign. (Twitter and Facebook postings, with the links.)

ITS FREE, you only have to learn to do it once. It could be the best time investment you ever make.

9.12   Other Advertising

Leaflets? Well, if you must. There is a place for leaflets and it's not through letter boxes! Leaflets with specific offers and new starter courses can be made to work very effectively but only if you can put them into the hands directly of your Target Market.... INTO THEIR HANDS.

Giving a prospective student (someone in your Target Market) a leaflet directly, and imparted with good friendly energy, gives the prospect a chance to see you are a human being who is warm and friendly; someone who is no longer a 'scary Black Belt' with whom contact might make them feel uneasy. In short, your leaflet should be a reminder of you after you have broken the ice.

9.13   Press Advertising

Paid for press advertising in newspapers etc, is expensive, short term and you might just get a large response. Can you handle 30 enquiries in one day? What if you hit the wrong week when something else bigger in the newspaper is happening, or if DFS launch yet another sale, your expensive ad can just be lost.

Fine if you can spend big and get the best spot in the paper; maybe you are planning some kind of Launch, but as on an on-going promotional tool, my opinion is that the other forms of advertising discussed are much more cost effective.

Magazine and Local Directories

I am aware of a small number of schools who advertise on a monthly basis in these magazines, some with more success than others. My opinion again, is that this is a scatter gun approach to advertising and should be given a miss. In my experience the cost per new student is extremely high.

9.14   Editorials

A no-cost editorial in a newspaper or magazine is fantastic; I love free validation of my Black Belt Business. In editorials I get to be positioned by the media as an expert and therefore my opinion is credible and worthy. I can advertise to my Target Market whilst not directly advertising; I can put across my values and beliefs, which of course match my Target Market's and so create interest and rapport with my target prospects. All that's needed then is my website details and we are on the way to more free students.

You've got to love editorials.

9.15 Marketing - to sum up

These are the most important sentences in the book (as well).

<u>Target your Target Market and make the most of the web and advertise all day every day for FREE.</u>

<u>Become an Expert at being Perceived as an Expert.</u>

Chapter 10   Programmes and Structure.

10.1   Complementary Programmes

Ok, I know, I know, you still want to attract more than one Target Market.

You can do exactly that with Complementary Programmes, but be aware that each programme lessens the effectiveness of your marketing. Don't fall into the trap of the scatter gun approach. If you want everything you may well get nothing.

So what I suggest is that you keep the main thing the main thing, but facilitate spin offs. If you run a children's Black Belt Business, then a Younger programme might be a good way forward. No, not an MMA set up, it's too far removed from what you do.

Younger children may well end up in the main children's programme.

The parents may wish to train so a mixed class might work well for you. As you market to parents, there may be some crossover to the children's classes so it seems at first glance to be a good call.

If you do MMA it might not be too far to run a grappling programme. This would attract students who may well cross over to your main programme. But to start a pensioners' programme is, in my opinion, folly.

Complementary Programmes can be excellent for your business but there are considerations.

What is the cost of doing another programme; what is the cost with this time slot being taken up with the new 6 students you've attracted, when you could have spent the marketing budget more effectively on attracting 20 students to your main activity?

What has been the opportunity costs (the things you didn't do while you were doing the new programme)?

Think long and hard before running to add more and more STUFF to the business. Complementary Programmes can be a great way forward, if they are that ... Complementary.

10.2   Class structure

I'm right back on my soap box now; this is the one subject that drives me to despair.

Separate your classes into clearly defined classes for clearly defined groups so you can get clearly defined results.

Five year old children do not want to train alongside fifteen year old crazy adolescent kids. Most women don't want to train alongside sweaty men. Beginners don't want to be shown up by experts. Green belts don't want to stand around while you teach a brown belt.

Your students:

Don't all want the same things from training
Don't all want the same atmosphere
Don't all want the same intensity
Don't all want to do the same things
Don't all want the same lesson
Don't all learn at the same pace
Don't all learn the same way
Don't all have the same values, needs, wants, interests
Don't all have the same physical abilities

10.3 STOP IT!

Stop treating Students

as if they are

all the Same,

Because they're Not.

STOP IT, STOP IT,

STOP IT.

Sorry about that. (I feel better now). So if you can't lump everyone into one class, what are you to do?

Well, split them by what they Want and Need. Sounds easy doesn't it?

Have a view to the time you have available to teach and a view to the students in your Target Market. If it's children's classes you run, then the classes can start after school, say from 4 o'clock (in the UK) and run until bed time (for most children with school the next day, 8:30 pm would be late).

If it's adults, it's after 'work and tea and family' time, so 7pm onwards may be fine.

I know if you are just launching then you will have no intermediate and advanced students, but you will (hopefully) have them one day and it'll be no good telling them they have to leave your business because you never planned-in any time to teach them at the start.

Saturday Mornings: Kids' times?

Sunday Mornings: Adult times?

As I said near the start of this book, there seems to be no specific time when you can't attract a Target Market to your Black Belt Business, differing times are sometimes better for different Target Markets, but it's your Business so teach when you want to teach; whatever floats your boat.

A daily progressive timetable seems to be as good as any I have come across - one which starts at 4:30 pm with young children then goes up by either age or grade through the evening, finishing with Beginner Adults then Advanced Adults from 9pm onwards.

But hey, it's just a suggestion.

10.4   So, how long is a lesson?

That depends on you; it's your Black Belt Business; it depends on who you are teaching and what you are teaching.

In the old days I used to train for 2 or 3 hours at a time, admittedly half of that was standing around *practising* in inverted commas (yes I meant to write 'in inverted commas'!). I think that is a hell of a long time for any meaningful lesson.

Today I think an hour's purposeful lesson is plenty and if you are teaching children, 45 minutes is a fairly long lesson. At school most lessons are 30 minutes. If you are teaching the under 6 year olds, a 30 minute lesson is a lifetime.

So again, it's a bit prescriptive of me but all under 6s, 30 minutes; and for 7 to 12 year olds, 45 minutes is plenty.

For 12 year olds and above, plus beginners, 45 minutes is fine (especially when you bear in mind the fitness levels of new students).

Advanced students over 12 and Intermediate Adults and above, 1 hour would be a good class for most.

Any down time between lessons is a waste of time and so a waste of money.

Between 5pm and 8pm you can fit in 3 one hour lessons at 20 students times your mat fee, or you can fit in four 45 minute lessons with 20 students times your mat fee. That's 25% more income in the same 'Prime Teaching Time'. Hey, it's your business.

If you are providing specific teaching for specific groups, then 45 minutes per class is perfectly acceptable. The teaching will be very effective for the group and there will be no time to get bored. Try it; you will never go back.

10.5   Class Control

Many schools operate a 'come as you please' pay policy for unlimited lessons. I'm not the biggest fan of this as it means the class size can vary dramatically. If the teaching one week is on a 1 to 8 ratio and then on a 1 to 35 ratio the next, this, in the eyes of the student (or his mother), is a school out of control.

I assign a student to a class and that's what he/she pays for..... that place. It adds credibility to be paying for a place in the school rather than just paying for direct instruction.

I know that sounds strange but it is important to keep the 'want' factor.

It also means absence from class does not trigger an "I want a refund" situation. I do, of course, allow catch up lessons for those who have been ill etc. but the student's membership entitles him/her to a place in the school, not the lesson.

It also helps with students who have a habit of taking long holidays for five weeks or so, perhaps to India or America. They might not be in attendance but they still have to pay for their place, or leave and re-join in the future (and pay the membership fee again). I'm not a money grabbing lunatic and of course, I use my discretion with this policy, but it is in place and if it wasn't, someone would take advantage of it. People, hey?

So my advice for what it's worth is to keep control of who is allowed to come and when. You can always cut people some slack, but you try reeling it back if someone is abusing your system and business!

10.6   Eight year old Black Belts. What the...... !!!

Ok guys, a sticky subject; horror for many people and a horror to me.

My feelings towards someone wearing a Black Belt when they couldn't protect themselves in real life is not to be repeated in a quality publication like this.

So, you earned your Black Belt the hard way. In the old days, it took you 5 years of graft. Blah, blah, me too.

What if you had put that same graft in but you started training when you were 5 or 6 years old? By the age of 10 you would have learned what you needed to get your Black Belt.

So you see the dilemma of an Instructor whose students start training at the age of 4. What do you do with them after 10 years of training?

What belt do they wear? If you take the syllabus of your Instructor from Back In The Day and apply it, after a time period you will run out of belts. Either that or you tell your students they can only grade every 24 months (hardly a recipe for motivation and student retention).

You need a new way; a new syllabus for children. At Team Black Belt we have 28 belts to get to an adult Black Belt, 24 of which require a minimum of 4 months' training and the last 4 require 9 months' training to qualify. It takes 12 years for a student to go from a 5 year old Little Dragon to an Adult Black Belt.

The student is constantly motivated to reach the next level. There is a clear progression path, and we don't have the embarrassment of a student with a Black Belt at the age of eight.

Sure, we have Little Dragon Black Belts and Junior Black Belts but a Team Black Belt Black Belt is reserved for those who can go out into the wider world and wear their Black Belt with pride and justification.

So, it's not the student's fault that they receive a Black Belt after 3, 4 or 5 years' training; it's not even the Instructor's fault, it is the fault of those running an Association or higher who didn't recognise that the old pre-war grading syllabus which had served well in the last century when Martial Arts were the domain of adults, had become a folly when today children start as young as 3 years old.

Rewrite your syllabus; make it easier and child friendly. We all know that the aim is a Black Belt (or above), but not to the non-Martial Artist, stop thinking like a Black Belt and make that goal the ultimate goal whilst giving the kids a chance to see progression and achievement. If you do, you can retain students for huge periods of time without selling out by giving away the Big One. You will end up with some magnificent students because if they keep coming, they will keep improving.

Oh, and just one other thing; if you know it will take 10 to 12 years for a student who joins at 4 years old to get to Black Belt, there is little need to pressure them into 'burning out' by training three times a week for 3 hour sessions is there? (Thus avoiding the need to discount your Hourly Teaching Rate for them by doing so.)

Chapter 11   Rotating Curriculum

11.1 What is a Rotating Curriculum?

A rotating curriculum is the most brain bending thing I have come across in my Martial Arts career; it is also the best teaching aid I have ever come across. I will do my best to explain it as best I can.

A rotating curriculum is where all the members of a class are taught the same thing at the same time. There, that wasn't too hard was it?

Well, that's ok in month 1 but what about month 2 if a new students joins? I will be teaching month 2 stuff to a month 1 student, ..oh and what about month 6 when a new student joins? Month 6 stuff to a month 1 student? Month 12 lessons to a month 1 student?

Well, I am not sure how to put this to you but, err, Yes! It may be that you are teaching a new student the same lesson as a month 12 or even a month 24 student…

Now that's got you; you think I'm a nut case. Well I'm not, so bear with me.

11.2 Advantages over Traditional

In a traditional set up, a student is taught in a linear pattern, with each step getting increasingly difficult, then at every new belt, it gets more difficult again, and so on.

This is fine if you just want to teach a few students in a class, and they don't mind standing around or 'practising on their own' as you teach a different student. Try teaching a kata or drill to one student and then different katas again to student No.2 and No.3.

You will teach the first student for 10 minutes and not get back to them for another 20 minutes (or you dodge about like a lunatic). It's why classes in the old days used to be 3 hours long; the teaching wasn't thought through, even if the Martial Art was.

So, a Rotating Curriculum teaches every student in the class *the same thing at the same time*. You teach all the students and they all get the benefit of your wisdom.

The question is, will a student who has trained with you for 6 months pick things up quicker and be able to perform them better than a month 1 student? Yes of course they will. You would expect an increased ability to both learn and perform what they are shown, over a beginner.

No 'dead time' in the class; all students get your teaching for all the class. If you explain a technical issue, they all get to hear and apply it.

Still not convinced? Your system is too complicated for that?.... NO it isn't.

It's just a new concept and it will take some working out. You need to think like a professional teacher, not like a Black Belt doing what you've always done.

Think of it as a modular way of teaching; Colleges often teach in this modular way so you can access the courses several times a year.

11.3 How to Create a Rotating Curriculum

This takes brain power; you have to think in a different way and that hurts.

Ok, I will use Team Black Belt as my reference so you can see what we have done. (I have simplified and changed our belt structure just so it's easier to understand.)

In the traditional linear way of grading, after 12 months a student would grade from white belt to yellow to orange to green

To gain a Yellow Belt a student might have to do a

Front Kick
Front Punch
Partner work 1

For Orange Belt

Round Kick
Reverse Punch
Partner work 2

For Green Belt

Side Kick
Hook Punch
Partner work 3

So, that's standard stuff. But during a lesson with 20 students of mixed grades, you are going to teach all of the above at every lesson, and everyone is going to get one third of the lesson on what they want to learn! Now if it is just three techniques for each grading then it's doable.

However, what if your syllabus requires 8 or 10 things for each grading? You will spend two thirds of each class teaching stuff to 'Other Students'.

Every lesson you ever do will vary depending on who turns up on any particular day, and what grade they are. Got a plan for that then?

If you accept that at the end of one year, a student who trains properly will know all the techniques in the curriculum (as outlined below), then it generally doesn't matter which order he learns them in, as long as he knows them. In reality and practice the modules are not that different in terms of difficulty to each other.

So instead of grading on a linear system, you can grade on a modular system. The old Yellow Belt syllabus would become a module, the old Orange Belt syllabus would become a module and the old Green Belt syllabus would be a module.

So now you award a belt for each module completed (knowing at the end of 12 months the student would have trained on all modules required for a Green Belt). They will still be a Green Belt, just a better one.

So, regardless of when a student starts, Term 1, Term 2 or Term 3, at the end of 12 months they will have completed 3 modules and be a Green Belt.

Therefore you can award a Belt per module completed.

Any 1 Module gets a Yellow Belt

Any 2 Modules gives you an Orange Belt

And 3 Modules gives you a Green Belt

For the example below, I have used 3 terms, however, your business could cover 3 or 4 terms.

January to April   (Module 1)
May to August   (Module 2)
September to December   (Module 3)

Therefore, a student who starts training in September would complete Module 3 in December but would not be awarded a Green Belt at the end of it. He would, for completing 1 module, receive his Yellow Belt.

He would then continue to train in the same class doing Module 1 in the January to April of next year, gaining his Orange Belt, then onto Module 2 in May through to August, finally then gaining his Green Belt.

The students who have completed 3 modules will be awarded their Green Belts and move to the Intermediates Class (the next time slot) where he will start the Year 2 modules, Blue, Purple, Red Belts and so on.

For every student, every minute of every lesson being taught is relevant for their next belt. They stay attentive and interested, and the whole group support each other and move forward together.

Does it work for Expert level students? This rotating curriculum works right the way up the grades. However, I go back to a more Linear method of grading for Brown and Black Belts where I place a greater degree of emphasis on personal performance. These people may have been with your school for many years, and you will be very aware of the training they need. They are also able to train and practise correctly whilst you teach someone else during a class.

11.4 Is it worth it?

It is a major undertaking to develop a rotating curriculum; it is however a fantastic way to control the progress of your school.

At Team Black Belt I can tell you what lesson a student will be taking any week from the day they join up to 8 years into the future.

I know that sounds a bit nerdy, but it is easy once the curriculum is in place. We just work out what is required for each Module for each Term and then break it into what is required on each week to get there. Easy.

By the way, I am far more spontaneous than I sound, as anyone who knows me will testify. I have built in Fun weeks, Competition weeks, Self Defence weeks and Non-Syllabus weeks.

Do I stick to it? Largely yes, but it's my Black Belt Business and my Plan and my Curriculum so if the mood takes me I swap a week around to suit me.

Just a thought; when I have my Leadership Team or Assistant Instructors take the reins, they know exactly what is required for each class they take; exactly where that lesson fits into the whole and so they don't need to run and ask me what to do every 5 minutes. Hey, I get some chill time!

It all builds towards the final outcome: an efficient, effective Black Belt Business that meets my needs, and works even when I'm not there.

Now that's what I'm talking about. Is it worth it?...... You'd better believe it!

11.5 Gradings - Everyone Passes!

So, if you have a revolving curriculum, the grading tests become much easier to arrange and control. Every Term or Module there is a grading for everyone in the class structure. Simples.

Now, a very controversial statement: **Everyone Passes.** Yes, I said it. I'm a heretic. My standards are poor; I will never be a Martial Artist. Wrong, wrong, wrong and wrong again.

If you have a syllabus in which it takes many years to achieve a Black Belt, then you have taken the time to break the syllabus out into manageable chunks, (modules), and then you teach everyone in the class those chunks for 13 weeks. **THEY SHOULD PASS** their grading.

If they haven't attended class (the minimum required by you to grade) then **they don't grade.**

If they have attended and done their best to learn what you have taught them then **they should pass**.

If they don't **you have let them down**. (Your syllabus is wrong; there is too much in it, or you expect too much in too short a time frame).

Students are relying on you to know what you are doing, and that you are qualified to teach it to them. If you don't or you can't, it's not for you to punish them and label them a failure. You need to look at what you do!

Will some students be in the top 10% for ability - YES

Will some students be in the bottom 10% for ability - YES

It means the rest are in the middle 80%

As long as the class is moving forward, everyone in the class will be moving forward.

So allow the class to do just that. Move forward. Everyone Passes!

If they really can't do what you are asking of them, politely pull them out of the grading a week or two before it takes place, and explain why.

11.6 What about Black Belt Gradings?

There comes a time in every Martial Artist's training when they become responsible for their own personal training and their own performance.

It isn't at Green Belt or Purple Belt level. However, by the time students get to somewhere near adult Black Belt testing they should understand it is their personal work rate and practise regime that is going to make the difference.

A student at the higher levels should have gone from being reliant upon you as the source of their performance, to being responsible for their own standards.

I fully support the pass/fail standards for these grades.

Oh look - more important sentences!

If your Junior students fail a Grading test, it is you who have failed them, you need to change what you are doing!

If a Senior student fails a grading test, they have failed you.

It is they that need to change what they are doing

Chapter 12   Control Your Business

12.1 Business Dashboard.

There are certain key issues that you need to know about your business in the same way that you need to know certain information in order to drive your car.

In your car you have a dashboard so you can check your speed; you have a rev counter so you can tell how fast the engine is revving; you have a 'what gear am I in' indicator to help you drive; a fuel gauge so you know to fill up before you run out, etc etc.

However, if you drive along staring at the dials it might be a bit tricky, so you should still be concentrating on the road!

For your Black Belt Business you will need a dashboard, and, like the dashboard in the car, you don't need to constantly stare at it, but it helps to give you an idea of how you are performing and if you should pay a bit more attention to one thing or another (like fuel or oil levels).

12.2 So what are the key indicators I need on my dashboard?

1   How many students do you have?

That sounds fairly simple, but I don't mean the total number that includes the non-paying places you allocate such as leaders, helpers or any charitable places you may have, I mean the number of students who pay every month.

2   Actual Monthly Billing

The total Mat fees collected through normal collection, excluding special events.

3   Average Billing per month, per student, last month

Your monthly fee income divided by the number of active students.

4   New enquires to join business

The total number of enquiries you received last month.

5   Number of trial students last month

The number of enquiries who turned up to do their trial lesson or lessons.

6   New students last month

How many of those trial lessons turned into enrolled students.

7   Number of 'lost' students

The number of students who have done their last lesson, i.e. leavers.

8   Monthly percentage retention (leavers / total students)

The number of leavers as a percentage of the total number of students.

9   Business capacity

The total number of places available in your Black Belt Business, if all your classes were full.

10   Monthly Break-even point

How much it costs you to be in business each month.

11   Monthly operating profit

Your monthly Billing minus your Break-even point.

12   Last month's forecasted Tax Bill

You need to check with your Accountant for this one; it depends on just how much money your business is earning. You should put an amount aside each month for the end of year tax bill. If you over estimate this amount, after your tax bill is paid you can pay yourself a bonus; but always take financial advice from a professional Accountant.

12.3   Information the Easy Way

So how do you get this information? You could sit up late at night with a calculator, and many schools do just that and there is nothing wrong with that. It's just that life is too short for me, and Key Performance Indicators is where my Management Company comes in. They have much of this information available at the click of a button.

I just sign into the system and there it is…. That's cool. Thank you NEST Management www.nestmanagement.com

I have control over my KPIs and over my business.

Chapter 13   Business Planning

13.1   Your Vision

Hopefully, you have a good idea of what your long term vision is and what you are trying to achieve; you have written it down at the start of this book.

What do you mean you still haven't?? Go back to the start and read the book again and this time, **do it!** It's <u>important</u> - if you don't know where you are going, you sure as heck can't get there.

13.2   5 Year Dream

I know trying to plan for anything 5 years away is tricky. I know you are sure that you can't be sure, and some of you may even be sure that you are sure to be wrong. That doesn't matter. Some bright spark had a dream many years ago to bring the Olympics to London and even started planning for it, and just look where that got us!

So you need to start to dream the future.

I am going to ask you to assume you could not fail and everything you touch will turn to gold.

In five years' time, what will your Black Belt Business look like?

Go on, pretend it's Christmas and you could have anything you want; pretend I'm your Fairy Godmother (steady) and I will grant you your Five year business dreams - but you have to tell me in writing what they are right now!

I will leave you a page to write it down. Remember, if you can't write it down in the next 10 minutes, you can't have your wish granted.

Come on, think. What's your 5 year dream……..?
How many schools have you got in five years?

How many students?

How many instructors work with you?

Are you in your own building? How many square feet?

Or are you in schools, colleges etc?

How many Black Belts are there?

Do you have your own Association or Style; system even?

What do your classes look like? Who's in them?

What else?

What does it mean to be part of your Black Belt Business?

Are you on the TV?

In Films, doing stunt work?

Think!, No not think......*Dream*! Come on; you have 10 minutes from now to write down what your Dream is - how things could be in five years' time.....

Set your timer. Turn to the next page, Ready... **GO!**

My Dream is that in Five Years' Time I will have a Black Belt Business which…

....
....
....
....
....
....
....
....
....
....
....
....
....
....
....
....
....
....
....
....

13.3 One Year Objectives

If you worked at a pace during the last section you will have written some great stuff and some, well shall I say, not so great stuff. So in this section we will look at taking the things we have written down in our Five Year Wish List, and see what you need to do in order to start moving forward.

Take your Five Year Dream and extract the things that you really are prepared to work for. The big three or four things that, if you achieved them, would make you feel fantastic; you'd be a success.

These big dreams are about to become your Goals, the things you are going to work towards.

Write them down in the space below. Don't bin the others because somewhere in your mind they have a place, (and, who knows, in a couple of years' time your priorities may change), we just need to get more focus so that we can move forward.

Write down the big 3 or 4 (or 6 - it's your dream!).

My five year goals are

Now what can you do to move significantly towards those five year goals, say, in the next 12 months? If you worked hard; if you went for it; what could you expect to have achieved by this time next year?

Where would you be?

Write it down.... Come on, write it down. Put the marker in the sand.

In Twelve Months' Time, that is by the ...... day of .... 20.....

I will have done, achieved or got....what? **GO!**

....
....
....
....
....
....
....
....
....
....
....
....
....
....
....
....
....

Brilliant, now you have something to aim for, a goal (or several hopefully). Now we are going to turn these goals into targets for you to meet.

What do you need to achieve in the next 3 months, or 90 days, that will ensure you are on target to score that twelve month goal?

My 90 Day Targets are

....
....
....
....
....
....
....
....
....
....
....
....
....
....
....
....

These 90 Day Targets become Mini Projects in their own right.

There will be stuff that must be done in a sequential order, or by a specific date.

So now plan your first 'Mini Project' into a timeline:

What must be done in   Month 1 (this month)
                       Month 2 (next month)
                       Month 3 (the last month in the 90 day cycle)

You now have 3 months of 'Must be done this Month'.

Take this month's 'Must be done this Month' list and assign each part to a weekly time line.

Must be done in week   1
                       2
                       3
                       4

You now have a 'Must be done this Week' list.

It doesn't take a rocket scientist to work out a "must be done today" list…..

You now have a time line which takes you:

From a 5 Year Dream to a 12 Month Objective

From a 12 Month Objective to a 90 Day Project

From a 90 Day Project to a 1 Month Deadline

From a 1 Month Deadline to a To do this Week

From a To do this Week to a Today's Activity

My Five Year Dream is to have 1200 students training with me. OMG!

(I am assuming, for the sake of this example, a consistent increase in the number of students throughout the five years).

In order to have 1200 students in 5 years' time, I need to recruit 240 new students a year for the next 5 years.

Again, assuming a constant growth rate, in 90 days' time I will need to attract a quarter of the 240 students required for this year, so I need 60 new students in the next 90 days.

This is my project for the 90 Days: You will need to do something to attract them, for example, give out 5000 flyers.

My 90 Day Project is to Attract 60 Students.

I anticipate that in order to attract 60 new students I need to distribute 5000 flyers.

My timeline for the project will look like this:

Month 1

Source a printing company.
Work with them to design a leaflet which pulls students in.
Collect leaflets (7 day wait).

Month 2

Talk to Head teachers at the local schools to see if they will help.
Distribute leaflets (5 days' work).
Take responses and arrange start dates.

Month 3

Set up trial lessons and sign up new students.

Now to break out the Monthly Deadline into the To do This Week.

Month 1 Week 1

Today I need to contact some printing companies, arrange meetings and obtain quotes.

Month 1 Week 2

Work with designers and approve leaflet design.

Month 1 Week 3

No work required on this project

Month 1 Week 4

Collect leaflets and begin distribution.

And break down the tasks from Weekly into Day by Day Action, e.g

Month 1 Week 1 - Monday: Today's activities

Work out a rough leaflet design

Month 1 Week 1 - Tuesday: Today's activities

Contact local printer companies
If you follow the process it looks like this:

My Five Year dream is to have 1200 students.

One year Goal is to have 240 students.

90 Day Target is to attract 60 students.

1 Month deadline is to distribute 1000 Flyers

This week's To Do is to order 1000 flyers from a printing company.

Today I must contact 3 printing companies for quotes.

I understand it's a long way off but the action I take today ie contacting 3 printing companies for quotes, is directly linked to my fantastical Five Year dream.

I know it, I've planned it and I want it. I am working to a plan to get me where I want to go. You can too.

You don't need me to be your Fairy Godmother.

Anyway, I would look terrible in a dress.

Chapter 14   Business Status

14.1 What kind of Company will you be?

I am not an Accountant and I am not qualified to write a chapter on accountancy stuff, but that never stopped me before, so here goes. Please check with your Accountant before doing anything.

If you're outside the UK, please feel free to read this section as it may raise issues and questions which are important to you but the answers in your particular jurisdiction will most likely be different.

Things to consider about your Black Belt Business:

Will you be Self Employed, in a Partnership, a Limited Liability Partnership or a Limited Liability Company?

There are several issues to consider when answering these questions.

1   What are the statuses above and what does each one mean to you?

You need to understand how each of the above statuses work, and the advantages and disadvantages of each. The size of your business may affect which way you go.

2   How does my insurance work in each of the above?

Public Liability and Professional Indemnity

You will need both types of insurance and the 'status' you choose will affect the cost and type of policy you require. Check it out.

3   What are the Tax implications of each of the statuses?

Limited liability companies are generally more complex to be in, and require more accounting, and therefore have more accounting costs, but may have some benefits too.

4   VAT?

In the UK, if you teach a Martial Art in your 'Own Right', the business may be exempt from charging VAT. If you have chosen to be a Limited Company you may not be regarded as teaching in your 'Own Right', as you will technically be employed by the Company you own.

Again, check it all out – there are lots of useful websites that will help you look into which way is the best way for you, or an accountant can offer you advice.

A Google search will give you all the results you need, a great starting point in the UK is the government set up advice site http://www.hmrc.gov.uk

Chapter 15   The Most Important Sentences.

The most important sentences in this book are

NOT

the ones I have written.

They are the ones

YOU

have written !

(But here are the ones I have written again......)

Money is the Representation of

VALUE

the more Value you give the more Money you Receive.

You can't Earn Money, you can only Give Value and in Return you Receive Money.

If your Students do not love attending your classes they will go and do Something Else.

If they do Something Else, you cannot teach them anything and they will pay you NOTHING!

Your Target Market Dictates Everything your Business does.

Everything Should be Aimed at Attracting and Retaining your Target Market.

Your Target Market

IS NOT, Is Not, is not

IS NOT !

just Anyone who

wants to train!

When you are the student, Your Needs, Feelings and Expectations should be met.

When you are the Instructor, it is your Students' Needs, Feelings and Expectations that you need to meet.

Your Income

is a Direct Result of

your Customers being Delighted

with what you do,

time after time

after time,

after time,

after time

after time!

You are going to Give More Value, to More People, than most will ever Give and you will Change Lives for the Better.

So be Proud of your Profession and be a Professional Instructor and Business Owner.

I will NOT accept Pay-as-you-Go students…Ever.

I will charge my students for their place in my class, not whether they attend or not.

I will use a Direct Debit Collection Service or Standing Orders.

If you are not

Actively Marketing

your Black Belt Business then

you are

Actively keeping it a Secret!

They 'Ain't Bothered' about you

or your past.

They Want, what They Want

and are asking you

"What's in it for me?"

Market to Their Wants not

Yours!

Target your Target Market and make the most of the web and advertise all day every day for FREE.

Become an Expert at being Perceived as an Expert.

Stop treating Students

as if they are all the Same.

Because they're Not.

STOP IT, STOP IT,

STOP. IT.

If your Junior Students fail a Grading test, it is you who have failed them - you need to change what you are doing!

If a Senior Student fails a grading test, they have failed you. It is they that need to change what they are doing!

Chapter 16 .... and one more thing!

If you have got this far through the book, I want to congratulate you and thank you. I know you are a Martial Artist and you can get through almost anything you set your mind to, but thank you anyway.

You may have agreed with everything in this book. If you have, you must be, like myself, one of the truly enlightened and I salute you! To some I am sure it has posed a few questions and ideas to which you are resistant. I have to say that's OK as well. My business approach may not be to everyone's taste but I can assure you the business principles outlined are sound.

With my own Black Belt Business we have tried to take the traditions and best practices of the Masters who came before us and build upon them.

As with all things, everything changes, and unless you are a Martial Artist who studies the oldest ways and adheres to them strictly as a way of preserving them in that form, then you must be open to change.

We live in different times, and in different countries with different cultures and I think we need to reflect on the way we do, what we do. If not, we run the risk of losing students to video screens and other distractions.

As I have said earlier in this book, Martial Arts has been wonderful to me in my lifetime. For me, promoting it to as wide an audience as possible seems like the right thing to do. Some students who join me still leave in preference for other sports, recreations and studies, but we have a wonderful retention rate and many students go on to become First Class serious Martial Artists, which the old school Instructors and Masters recognise.

We have replaced the old ways of punching a board wrapped in straw until your hands bled, with an energy charged bright Dojo, with happy sweating students, learning, laughing and having a great time; which has led to them wanting to know more, do more, become physically fitter and stronger, and even, strangely enough, try that board and straw punching.

If I can encourage people to join me in my passion for Martial Arts, they have a lifetime to explore the things I don't teach, or don't even know. I do know, however, that before they spend a lifetime in Martial Arts, they have to fall in love with it.

So that's my aim - to get people to fall in love with what I do, and pay me for the privilege. I get to see human beings at their best, to see them challenged and respond to that challenge. I get to be a part of their growth and I get to see the values and beliefs that Martial Arts can instil into both the old and the youth of today.

If you are thinking of building a Black Belt Business I can't recommend it highly enough.

Addendum

I want to include a small section on Team Black Belt and our future plans.

I created Team Black Belt seven years ago (at the time of writing) with my partner Helen. I specialise in teaching Karate to children and Helen specialises in brilliantly running and organising the business.

All of the things I have written about in the book are in operation at Team Black Belt, but there is still more. We have in place a life lessons/skills programme: a full curriculum with lesson plans, week by week, which can take a five year old child through 'Little Dragon' Black Belt to Karate Kids, and through a seven year development programme to Junior Black Belt then onto Senior Black Belt a few years later.

(Older kids, as with Mums and Dads, join the programme later in the system and so progress quicker.)

We have a full Anti-Bullying Workshop - Stop Bullies NOW! with an affiliate programme for Martial Arts Instructors. Further info can be found at www.stopbulliesnow.org

We have marketing programmes and class support systems - in short we have developed a 'Black Belt Business in a Box'. We are now looking to work with a number of

Martial Arts Instructors who see the value in having someone else, (me), who has done the work before, help them with kick starting their Black Belt Business.

I am not looking to take people out of their current Association, nor for them to disregard their past, or disrespect their current Instructor, but if you are looking to build your Black Belt Business, either existing or from new, and you want to know more about the coaching I can offer, then I would be happy to hear from you.

If you have enjoyed this book and have any feedback on its contents, please do not hesitate to contact me.

(If you have hated this book, I apologise for wasting your time and money, please feel free to not contact me!)

I mean no disrespect to any Martial Art or System; I have gained too much from my training to do so, I just think it's time to come into the 21st century.

Once again thank you for reading my book, if you think I can be of further help to you or your Black Belt Business, Please feel free to get in touch.

Many thanks.

Michael Turbitt

Mike@teamblackbelt.com

Index

A

About Us' · 137
Alex Ferguson · 36
Amateur · 20
avoids · 100

B

Barry Tatlow · 11, 14, 18, 21
beliefs · 13, 22, 29, 30, 65, 141, 202
Black Belt · 1, 2, 3, 11, 13, 17, 19, 20, 22, 30, 31, 33, 34, 36, 37, 38, 42, 43, 44, 45, 46, 47, 48, 50, 53, 54, 55, 58, 59, 60, 61, 64, 65, 66, 67, 72, 74, 81, 85, 88, 90, 91, 92, 93, 94, 95, 98, 99, 100, 102, 103, 105, 109, 110, 111, 112, 113, 117, 118, 119, 123,124, 126, 130, 132, 133, 135, 137, 139, 140, 141, 143, 147, 148, 151, 152, 156, 160, 161, 163, 166, 168, 171, 172, 173, 184, 196, 201, 203, 204, 205
Black Belt Business · 1, 2, 3, 13, 20, 22, 30, 31, 33, 34, 36, 37, 42, 43, 44, 45, 46, 47, 48, 50, 53, 54, 55, 58, 59, 60, 61, 64, 65, 66, 67, 72, 74, 81, 85, 88, 90, 91, 92, 93, 94, 95, 98, 99, 100, 102, 103, 105, 109, 110, 111, 117, 118, 119, 123, 124, 126, 130, 132, 133, 135, 137, 139, 141, 143, 147, 148, 160, 161, 166, 168, 171, 172, 173, 184, 196, 201, 203, 204, 205
born to do · 19
Break-even · 168, 169
budget · 17, 109, 118, 144
buses · 17

business · 11, 15, 16, 17, 18, 19, 20, 22, 23, 33, 34, 37, 38, 43, 44, 46, 47, 48, 49, 50, 53, 54, 58, 64, 65, 66, 67, 70, 78, 84, 85, 86, 90, 93, 94, 95, 102, 103, 105, 109, 111, 118, 137, 144, 147, 149, 150, 158, 166, 167, 168, 169, 171, 185, 201, 204
Business Syllabus · 43

C

Cabbages · 25
cannon fodder · 37
Category 'A' Students · 64
Category 'B' Students · 64
Category 'C' Students · 64
Category 'D' Students · 64
Check · 83
Chickens · 24, 25, 26, 32
Christmas · 171
Clarity · 46
Class Control · 149
Clothing · 31
Contract · 16
convenient · 32
courses · 2, 18, 111, 140, 156
court · 17

D

dead time · 156
Diane Jarvis · 10
discount · 32, 116, 117, 118, 153
DJ · 105
Dojo · 14, 15, 18, 19, 21, 22, 98, 99, 101, 202
Doug Sedgley · 11
dream · 170, 171, 174, 182

E

editorial · 141
Elite · 51, 61, 67, 109
Equipment · 32, 105
exchange · 24, 30, 84

F

Fee structures · 115
free-standing · 105

G

garage door · 114
golf club · 31
Gradings · 30, 161, 163
Graham Tuckey · 10
Grand Master · 34, 58
Gym Memberships · 114

H

head guard' · 3
Helen · 11, 204
Hobby · 35

I

Ian McCrannor · 10
indestructible · 113
investment · 2, 3, 68, 89, 98, 105, 140
invitation · 18, 116

J

Jaguar Cars · 15
Julia Roberts · 11

K

Karate · 10, 11, 12, 14, 15, 17, 18, 19, 33, 54, 72, 90, 93, 204
kick bag · 105
Kids · 147, 204
Kung Fu · 33

L

leaflets · 140, 180, 181
Leases · 16
Life skills · 109
Limited · 16, 184, 185
Location · 97

M

Martial Artists · 2, 3, 13, 20, 35, 37, 88, 108, 126, 129, 133, 202
Membership · 31
meta tags · 138
Michael Turbitt · 3, 13, 205
Micro Location · 102
Mission · 90, 91, 92, 93, 94, 95, 98, 103
monetary value · 13, 32, 53
money · 2, 13, 16, 19, 24, 25, 26, 30, 32, 35, 38, 49, 53, 93, 95, 98, 100, 102, 113, 115, 117, 118, 119, 149, 150, 169, 205

N

Nest · 120
nestmanagement · 119, 169
Nigel Davison · 11, 18

O

old-school · 37

P

paper · 22, 52, 55, 141
Partnerships · 16
philanthropic · 47, 48
Pictures · 133, 136
Premises · 16
PRIMARY · 47
Professional · 20, 35, 39, 92, 107, 112, 185, 194

R

rain · 99
ranking · 138
respect · 12, 39, 53, 58, 73, 100, 110
retention · 60, 102, 105, 151, 168, 202
Round House kick · 22

S

Saturday · 110
Self Defence · 51, 54, 72, 78, 90, 160
selfishly · 49
Selling · 113
shame · 37
Shiomitsu · 18
skull and cross-bones · 130
social media · 138, 139, 140
Social proof · 137
Somali pirate · 130
STOP IT · 146
Stress · 16
Success System · 43
Sunday · 110, 147
Suzuki · 14
Syllabus · 43, 44, 45, 160

T

Takamizawa · 15
Target Market · 56, 57, 58, 59, 60, 63, 67, 71, 73, 75, 78, 79, 80, 82, 85, 86, 95, 97, 98, 110, 111, 116, 126, 127, 132, 133, 135, 136, 137, 139, 140, 141, 142, 143, 147, 190, 191, 198
THEY AIN'T BOTHERED · 129
traditional · 133, 134, 155, 156
tree · 19

U

Uncle Barry · 12

V

Value · 27, 28, 29, 30, 32, 106, 112, 114, 188, 194
VAT · 16, 185
venues · 100
video · 136, 137, 139, 201
Videos · 136
Vision · 46, 54, 81, 90, 91, 92, 94, 95, 170

W

Wado · 18
website · 134, 136, 138, 141
World Class · 11, 13, 19, 20
worth · 25, 54, 72, 108, 113, 114, 116, 150, 160, 161